GROWING INTO UNION

UNION

*Proposals for forming a united
Church in England*

C. O. Buchanan
E. L. Mascall
J. I. Packer
The Bishop of Willesden

D1421613

London
S·P·C·K
1970

First published in 1970 by S.P.C.K.
Holy Trinity Church, Marylebone Road, London N.W.1

Printed in Great Britain
at the University Printing House, Cambridge

SBN 281 02487 1

Contents

3

CONTENTS

The Authors

THE REVEREND COLIN OGILVIE BUCHANAN was born in 1934, and read Greats at Oxford. He was ordained in 1961. Since 1964 he has been first Librarian, then Registrar, of the London College of Divinity (which in Summer 1970 becomes St John's College, Nottingham). He has been a member of the Archbishops' Liturgical Commission since 1964. In 1968 he edited the reference work *Modern Anglican Liturgies, 1958–68*. His special interests are liturgical, sacramental, and ecumenical theology. He is an Evangelical.

THE REVEREND ERIC LIONEL MASCALL was born in 1905, and was a Wrangler in mathematics at Cambridge. He taught mathematics for some years, and was ordained in 1932. He is a Doctor of Divinity of Oxford, Cambridge, and (honorary) St Andrews, and since 1962 has been Professor of Historical Theology in the University of London at King's College. He is the author of many major works of theology, including *He Who Is* (1943), *Christ, the Christian and the Church* (1946), *Existence and Analogy* (1949), *Christian Theology and Natural Science* (1956), *Via Media* (1956), *The Secularisation of Christianity* (1965), *Theology and the Future* (1968), and those listed on pp. 192 and 212–13. He is a member of the Joint Theological Commission on Covenanting for Unity and of the Faith and Order Committee of the Missionary and Ecumenical Council of the Church Assembly. His particular concern is systematic and philosophical theology. He is a Catholic.

THE REVEREND JAMES INNELL PACKER was born in 1926, and read Greats and then Theology at Oxford, gaining his D.Phil. in 1954. He was ordained in 1952. From 1961 to the end of 1969 he was first Librarian, then Warden, of Latimer House, Oxford. In January 1970 he became Principal of Tyndale Hall, Bristol. His writings include *Fundamentalism and the Word of God* (1958), *Evangelism and the Sovereignty of God* (1961), and *God has Spoken* (1965). He was a member of the Anglican–Presbyterian Conversations 1962–5 and of the Anglican–Methodist Unity Commission 1965–8. He is a member of the Archbishops' Commission on Christian Doctrine and of the Faith and Order Committee of the Missionary and Ecumenical Council of the Church Assembly. His interests include systematic and historical theology, especially the Reformed and Puritan tradition. He is an Evangelical.

THE RIGHT REVEREND GRAHAM DOUGLAS LEONARD was born in 1921 and read Natural Science at Oxford. He was ordained in 1947. In 1964 he was consecrated Suffragan Bishop of Willesden in the diocese of London. He is Chairman of the Church of England Committee for Diocesan Moral and Social Welfare Councils and a member of the Church of England

Board for Social Responsibility and of the Legal Board of the Church Assembly. His theological interests are the communication of the gospel (on which he has contributed to various publications) and sacramental theology. He is a Catholic.

THE REVEREND EDWARD MICHAEL BANKES GREEN, who has contributed to two Appendixes, was born in 1930 and ordained in 1957. He is Principal of the London College of Divinity (St John's College, Nottingham) and author of many books, evangelistic and theological. He is an Evangelical.

Acknowledgements

Thanks are due to the following for permission to quote from copyright sources:

Geoffrey Chapman Ltd: *Ministers of Christ and his Church*, by David N. Power, O.M.I.

Collins Publishers: *The Stripping of the Altars*, by D. M. MacKinnon.

"Catholicism" and "Evangelicalism" are not two separate things which the Church of England must hold together by a great feat of compromise. Rightly understood, they are both facts which lie behind the Church of England and, as the New Testament shows, they are one fact. A church's witness to the one Church of the ages is a part of its witness to the Gospel of God.

The Archbishop of Canterbury, *The Gospel and The Catholic Church*, 2nd edn (Longmans 1956), p. 208.

Introduction

We write in the wake of the collapse of the Anglican–Methodist Scheme for unity, in order to offer an alternative way forward in the union of the Churches in England. This is avowedly inspired by the times through which we have recently lived, and it is impossible to look forward without at the same time learning from past mistakes and avoiding previous errors. We write too as definite Catholics and Evangelicals thrown together, as we shall show, almost entirely under the impact of events we neither sought nor welcomed.

This might suggest that we have conceived our task as "political". Surely Catholics and Evangelicals can write theology together at any time undisturbed by events, and with the leisure which is suitable to such a task but obviously lacking from this book? We gently disagree. Theology is occasioned (though not, we trust, wholly determined) by events. Which of Jeremiah, St Paul, St Athanasius, St Augustine, Martin Luther, John Henry Newman, or Karl Barth could have written theology as he did in any other circumstances? If no more, we are like them at least to this extent, that nothing but extreme necessity could have produced this book. It is a book which will never appear as other than a product of autumn 1969. But its task is a profoundly theological one. For it is theological thinking and reasoning which best serve men on this earth here and now. And a combination of Catholics and Evangelicals could, we dare assert, only be brought to the pitch we have reached in this task by the needs of the times as they have forced themselves upon us.

We believe the task to be not only timely but also honourable to undertake. We cannot accept any suggestion that there is something dishonourable in men who have apparently been opposed to each other seeking to discover how far this is really so. It is as men concerned to be consistent with ourselves as well as relevant to the times that we have undertaken this task. It has been for us not only a matter to be undertaken with a good conscience, but, far more than that, a matter of joy and mutual benefit in the experience. These facts would have been so even if (which we have logically had to face) the task had proved ultimately beyond us. That it has not done so, if we may so judge of our work, is a cause for thanksgiving over and above the fruits of sheer working together.

We take more seriously the possible reaction of other readers. Is not this yet another "inward-looking" theological book, to join the thousands of others, in which an ever-growing army of writers addresses an ever-decreasing platoon of readers? Are not these times which call for an "outward-looking" stance on the Church's part? And, if so, ought not this to command prior attention from those who would write? With these probing questions we have much sympathy, and acknowledge their insistent demand for an answer. We have felt it in ourselves.

The answer lies with others, not us. We have had to take up arms on fields others have chosen, not we ourselves. And yet on the one hand we do not regret this, and on the other we think it possible to move on from it. We do not regret it, because we believe there are still "inward-looking" tasks to be done, and the nature of the Church and its unity *in practical terms* is a crying theological priority. We cannot skip theology to address ourselves to the world, and here is a task not irrelevant to what we have to say to the world and how we have to say it.

We do not equate an outward union of the Churches with mission, nor do we imagine that union could guarantee success in mission. We do not commit ourselves to the claim that the quest for union must have priority as we seek church renewal in these days. We have listened, we hope sympathetically, to the voices which cry up unity as the palliative for all the Churches' ills, including their failure of nerve and lack of message, but we do not find ourselves convinced by them. The suggestion that the general paralysis of the Church today is the direct result of its internal division seems to us a patent rationalization of failures with far more deep-seated causes. In any case, we judge that the theological question of unity is misconceived and trivialized when church union is viewed and valued primarily as a means to an end. So our interest in the ending of scandalous division within God's family does not depend on any estimate of what consequences this might have in the other fields (where its effects might well be only marginal, and even if more would be purely contingent results under the hand of God). Rather, we see the achieving of visible oneness as necessary simply because it is the revealed will of God.

Results of obeying God's command can and must be left to God himself; they may never be transmuted into purposes on a basis of pragmatic calculation. We therefore take up the quest for union, not as a calculated pick-me-up for flagging Churches, but as a matter of plain Christian obedience. It is not, indeed, a quest that can be isolated from the quest for truth, and holiness, and faithfullness in mission, which God also commands, but equally it is not a quest that can be shelved while these other goals are pursued. The nature of the Church and of its God, and his revealed plan for his own people and for all mankind, make the quest for visible oneness an objective, which the Church in every age must seek. And because visible oneness is to be sought solely for God's honour, the means to it that are proposed must be honouring to God in their own right. No pragmatic cutting of the corners of principle is permitted here.

Yet, although this is the field we unashamedly occupy, we well know the need to move the contest on as soon as this field is secure. There is no point in labouring our duty to be outgoing in mission. It is acknowledged on all fronts as never before. Have we then prepared for this shift of ground? We think we have. Whereas the Anglican–Methodist Scheme focused only organizational and administrative reshuffles, we have sought to relate actual union of local churches to their task of mission. What by definition could not be our direct immediate objective has been, as far as we could make it so, a great indirect purpose of what we have written. We are confident that this will emerge in the reading.

THE ECUMENICAL SITUATION IN ENGLAND TODAY

Our previous remarks pinpoint the failure of the recent Scheme. It went wrong at conception and birth, and no amount of later aftercare could alleviate its congenital defects. We were thus offered a unity scheme without content, as far as Stage Two was concerned, without cost (except to the very conscientious) as far as Stage One was concerned, and without real participation in the decision as far as over 90% of the two Churches were concerned. We have spelled out elsewhere[1] what we conceive to have been the mischievous effects of following Lord Fisher's lead. We deal in passing elsewhere in this book with other defects. But it is germane at this

---

[1] See pp. 125 ff. and 171.

point to trace out the particular blunders which have led to the recent unpleasant cul-de-sac experience.

The first and most obvious is the head-in-the-sand decision-taking procedures in both Churches in 1965. The Convocations were confronted with very lukewarm support from round the country. Their committee which sat on the returns from the country was packed with the original signatories of the 1963 Scheme. The committee's report shows two things. First, statistically, out of 41 dioceses which had voted at some level on whether the Scheme offered "in broad outline" the way ahead, 8 had less than 50% support, 8 more had less than 65%, and 6 more less than 75%. Secondly, politically, the committee was determined just the same to recommend the Scheme, and did so by treating "yes" votes as responsible and mature and by discounting "no" votes as uninformed and due to misunderstanding. This was a most alarming piece of committee paternalism.

The Convocations themselves, at their joint session in May 1965, were afflicted by an astonishing euphoria about unity. Speaker after speaker outbid each other to commit the Church of England to as favourable a stance as possible towards the Scheme. Hardly a handful were prepared to voice or vote opposition. The Scheme was gratuitously handed extra years of life without the requisite support in the dioceses.

The Methodist Conference, which is more conscious of the power it holds, had little hesitation in voting by a 77% majority to adopt the broad outline (a two-stage scheme, the taking of episcopacy into Stage One, and a Service of Reconciliation to inaugurate Stage One) in July 1965. Yet the circuit quarterly meetings had only been in favour by 53% to 47%. Both Churches had now acted decisively at the centre without being dismayed by the division of opinion which had arisen in the country.

Exactly the same process was repeated in 1969, though with one or two additional items to lend drama to the picture. Evangelicals and Anglo-Catholics alike had indicated since the Interim Report of 1967 that they would have to oppose the Scheme. The 1969 diocesan and circuit returns *may* have been marginally more favourable to the Scheme than in 1965, but they fell far short of massive support. What the Church of England had been unable to do in the case of liturgy, it now proposed to do over reunion. In the case of liturgy, where the conscience of Evangelicals had been involved in the authorizing of Second Series Communion in 1967, the House of Laity (which had powers in this respect) had read sense into the Convocations and forced the abandonment of divisive features of change. When the even more far-reaching question of reunion, which affected the conscience of both Catholics and Evangelicals, came up for final consideration, the House of Laity had only advisory powers. The divisive nature of the Scheme duly emerged in the House's debates and voting, and the Laity accordingly passed a motion asking the Convocations to look for a new way forward[1]—but in the debate in Convocation this was ignored, and to date has never been tackled by the Convocations.

To the House of Laity figure was added the "referendum" return,[2] indicating that 37% (or 5,621) of the clergy were not prepared to take part in the Service of Reconciliation. To some of us on the sidelines it then seemed certain that the Convocations would have to agree that the Scheme could not be implemented, and to try to find some other way forward. To our amazement, despite the dignified and compelling stand of the Bishop of Carlisle (whose speech was memorable) and of some others, the Convocations addressed themselves to the task as though, broadly speaking, no evidence of support or lack of it from the country would make any difference. The House of Laity figures were derided, the "referendum" scorned. Opponents were blithely informed that they would change their minds once the Scheme was through, and hence their opposition could be discounted. And on this sort of basis the whole charade was acted through as though the element of divisiveness in the country could be voted out by two gross of clergy in Convocation. And yet, even this was a vain hope. A just sufficiently large percentage within the Convocations (largely elected members) were either themselves opposed to the Scheme or took the realistic view that the Scheme was not viable, inasmuch as "no" votes had to be treated as being as responsible and as serious as "yes" ones. The required 75% majority vote was not forthcoming.[3]

The Methodist Conference, meeting in Birmingham at the same time, was even less handicapped by attention to the lower levels of voting. Whereas the Anglican Convocations at least saw attempts

---

[1] For the text of this see p. 209.
[2] This sounding of clerical intentions was not strictly a constitutional referendum and the misnomer has led to bad publicity. Hence our quotation marks.
[3] The statistics are set out in full in Appendix 6, pp. 208–10.

to appeal from the House of Laity and the "referendum" to the lay voting in the diocesan conferences, the Methodist returns provided no such convenient evidence of a supposed groundswell in favour of the Scheme. But the task of the Conference is to give a lead, and give a lead the Conference did. And, at the time of writing, their lead must be followed through by a further round of voting in May Synods and the return of this "provisional legislation" to the 1970 Conference. If the required 75% is again available in summer 1970 then the Methodist Church will take up a most curious stance. On the one hand the Conference might appear to put its connexion into the position of a wallflower—ready for offers but receiving none. On the other hand, however, the wallflower will exercise moral pressure upon the Church of England to reconsider *its* position, and from that standpoint the Methodist Church qualifies not so much for sympathy in her embarrassing predicament as for circumspection in a situation where she might embarrass us.

For live as the issue may still be in Methodism (and the pages of the *Methodist Recorder* might make us question even that), it is almost dead in the Church of England. The Church of England throughout has continued to work at the reform of its Canon Law, its liturgy, its synodical forms of government, its theological colleges, its appointments to the ministry and a host of other matters without reference to the other Churches of this country. Despite certain dramatic insistences that the whole world was watching our decision on 8 July with bated breath, it has therefore been possible after the decision for the Church of England to continue on its rather aimless way without any disturbance of composure. What was a three days' wonder in the national press was perhaps a six weeks' one in the religious journals. But the general opinion seems now to be that it has not made much difference. And this was simply to be expected from a Scheme which might attract a lot of votes but involved no clear cost to the voters. There was no dying to live in Stage One, so there was very little sense that not to proceed to it was to oppose the will of God. Many Anglicans were unaware the 8 July decision was even being taken, and many more viewed it with very detached and correspondingly ephemeral interest. It is therefore a proper question as to whether any reintroduction of the Scheme could ever achieve that moral accord and acclaim which it would need to become viable. It seems more likely that the dismal parallel with the 1927–8 Prayer Book would be acted out to the final bathos where the second failure was heavier numerically but less memorable as a climax than the first.[1]

Nevertheless, the passing away of the Scheme has left a significant vacuum. Our duty to seek the union of the Churches is not diminished. The opportunity to find a viable way has reappeared after the years in which one scheme only was allowed on the table. The Church of England should buy up the opportunity. Does the House of Laity's resolution of 7 June 1969[2] still stand before the Convocations?

THE AUTHORS' HISTORY AND CREDENTIALS

As individuals we have been strongly orientated in one way or another over against the Scheme ever since February 1963. It has always bulked large in our attentions, and we have felt increasingly as individuals that we had to wrestle with the problems it set us. Our convergence into being a closely knit group writing a book in common can be traced back some time. There existed a strong friendship between the two Catholics and between the two Evangelicals for years before the bond was established across the party divide. It has been the years since 1965 which have seen the growth of this bond, and it may be helpful to trace out the stages.

The Bishop of Willesden and Colin Buchanan served together on the ill-fated Anglican–Methodist Council for Unity from 1966 to 1968. The only useful thing that Council ever did was to convene in June 1967 a residential conference for dialogue between supporters and opponents (both Anglican and Methodist) of the interim report *Towards Reconciliation* under the chairmanship of Dr Leslie Brown, Bishop of St Edmundsbury and Ipswich. Here we first found real sympathy with each other's position intellectually and spiritually as well as emotionally. Here too we encountered the

---

[1] This parallel, which some of us had voiced in public ourselves, was forcefully made in a speech by Prebendary Riley (a signatory of the 1963 Report) on 8 July. Quite apart from the question of two attempts he pointed to the history of over twenty years lying behind each event and the joining of Catholics and Evangelicals in opposition to each. He went on to point out how relieved the whole Church of England was (with the benefit of hindsight) that the 1927–8 Books had not been authorized. May we not have similar hindsight about the late Scheme?

[2] See Appendix 6, p. 209.

solid theological principle motivating the best of Methodist dissent. It was a turning-point. Thereafter the Bishop and Colin Buchanan were in intermittent contact about the Scheme.[1]

1967 also saw recognition thrust upon us by the official Unity Commission. When this Commission ran out of ideas and went into a slough in summer 1967 they asked various opponents of the interim report to appear before them. Dr Packer was of course a member of the Commission, who later signed a minority report.[2] The other three all appeared before the Commission[3] and gave evidence from their differing standpoints. The interesting thing to all four of us ourselves is that as we reconsider the statements we then made we each find this book to stand squarely in linear succession to them.

If the makings of a unified approach were there, we were ourselves still largely unconscious of it, and this we fully confess. The first real pulling together occurred when Michael Green served as a consultant at the Lambeth Conference of 1968, and found himself participating fairly fully in the section on which the Bishop of Willesden served. The Commission's final report was before the Lambeth Conference, and as those who had strong personal interest in it they found themselves in discussion. On the basis of this a first meeting was held in October 1968 which was attended by the Bishop, Michael Green, Colin Buchanan, Dr Packer, and Dr Morna Hooker, a Methodist dissentient. The theological discussion at this preliminary stage showed the way events would develop between us. It was impossible to discuss the Scheme in detail as we were constantly driven back to first principles.

Further meetings proved difficult to arrange, and perhaps in busy lives we did not see clearly enough the high priority they ought to have had. But by the spring of 1969 there were further factors to drive us together. One was the apparent determination by the powers that be in both Churches to write off all voting statistics which did not favour the Scheme. The second was the last-ditch argument in its favour, that its opponents were so divided that it was impossible to move the Scheme a step in the direction of one opponent without taking it further from another. This argument advertised the bankruptcy of theological commendation of the Scheme, but it was the counsel of despair, and should have been

---

[1] E.g. one of us wrote to the other on 1 September 1967, "I should think the scheme is now dead, and so one starts to plan for the vacuum beyond it."
[2] *The Scheme*, pp. 182–3.   [3] *The Scheme*, p. 2.

recognized as such. It was, however—and for this we thank God—the extra thrust needed to make us find time for each other.

Meetings of twos and threes (including Michael Green) preceded our May Statement[1] to the Convocations. There was every incentive to try to find an alternative scheme quickly, but as before we found it impossible to start discussion at this level. Driven back to first principles we were encouraged by the degree of agreement we found, but it became obvious to us that we had to give such time to clarifying our positions that we were unable to come up immediately with a ready-made set of proposals. We knew the political value that an alternative would have, but we were unable to cut corners to get there. We thus gave hostages to fortune in putting our hands first to the May Statement, then to the July one,[2] without such an alternative. For in those Statements we appeared not as men casually thrown together by a cynical concern (for diametrically opposed reasons) to have the Scheme rejected so that we might go back to our traditional stances. Rather we pledged ourselves to stay together, to work together, and not at any stage to settle for a way through which would satisfy one "side" whilst hurting the other. We think now that the two Statements, viewed against their public history and our private encounters, read as daringly as could ever have been expected in those circumstances. They have also proved to give exactly the guidelines we needed for the larger work we have undertaken since.

After the July vote we met briefly before two of our members departed for some time to South Africa and Australasia. This left the other two[3] to continue the work, and the fruit of this, with further promise of the whole group's continuing the major task, appeared in *Theology* for October 1969.[4] The whole group did not reassemble to continue its task until 3 October 1969. We now present our work as those who are still definitely and confessedly Catholics and Evangelicals, even as strong and uncompromising men of such persuasions. But equally we are not what we were. There has been a joy and a mutual benefit in tackling this task together, and we shall not lightly lose their impact.

[1] Printed here as Appendix 1 on p. 163.
[2] Printed here as Appendix 2 on p. 169.
[3] Michael Green, for reasons of his own time-table, had been unable to continue as a full member of the Group. He has remained in fullest sympathy with the project and results.
[4] Reprinted here as Appendix 3 on p. 176.

THE PROCEDURES FOLLOWED

The abortive starts we made in looking for alternatives, quite apart from some very unpleasant things said about us in public, have driven home to us the importance of method in writing a book like this. It will be helpful to set out the priorities of method to which we have been committed.

1. *The Primacy of Theology and Integrity.* We could not build without foundations. Hence the major part of our talking together has been about theology, and our book has had to start with fairly full discussion of the basic theological questions that the quest for unity raises, so as to lay a basis for practical proposals. We would not put up a building unless we could all take our place in it with good conscience. We have constantly appealed to our consciences (and to any corporate conscience there might be in the Church of England) as the personal expression of our objective theological standpoint. We could not act contrary to our own theologies. We have now therefore sought to take equal account of each other's theology and conscience, and this concern lies behind every practical proposal we make. Nor are we less concerned about the conscience of those who do not occupy exactly our own theological position, and we think they will find themselves able to approach our proposals with at least as good a conscience as they have in the Church of England today—often with a better.

2. *A Determination to go as far as possible.* Just as we knew in May and July 1969 that we could not provide a scheme without foundations, we have equally known since that, however good our foundations, we must not merely register theological agreements without clear indications of how to build on them. We therefore do offer the clear outlines of a scheme. Naturally we could not possibly answer all questions, whether theological or practical, that might be asked us. In three months of lives that are already full to the brim there is only a certain amount that can be done. But we have aimed to answer the key questions at some length, and are hopeful that these attempts indicate that more peripheral questions would also admit of satisfying answers. At some points we have made contingent suggestions for the implementation of particular proposals, and here other answers might do as well. But

we have tried to make clear that such suggestions are contingent, and in the main the structure of the book and of our thinking is not dependent upon them.

3. *An Organic Approach.* The whole book (excepting only those contingent points mentioned above) stands as a single whole. It is impossible to turn to one chapter, select one line of thought, and treat it as a piece of theological flotsam which might be driven up on any or no shore. The book has grown organically from the foundation chapters (plus a realistic appraisal of the present situation), and its proposals cannot be detached piecemeal and incorporated into other schemes with a bland assurance that we shall still recommend them. Other schemes are by no means excluded—indeed they are actively sought—but they must be rethought entire without any automatic assumptions culled from one part of this book.

4. *A Univocal Approach.* The writing of the book has been hasty, with all four of us drafting simultaneously. The results are inevitably rough, but we have been concerned above all that they should be honest, and we believe ourselves entitled to claim that this has been achieved—more effectively, perhaps, than if smoothness and polish had been the limit of our aims. We have not kept any controversial subject off our agenda, but have met any of which we were aware head-on. Equally, we have not then decided to omit any subject from the book. If there are omissions of controversial doctrinal matters it is by pure oversight, not suppression. And, even more important, we are not aware of any place where we can be taken in two different senses. Above all, we are not aware of having anywhere drafted anything with the deliberate intention that it should be taken in two senses. We do not defend ambiguity as a virtue. We have individually at times denounced the particular use of ambiguity by the late Scheme as dishonest. We have therefore scrupulously tried to avoid it ourselves.

In short we are all four committed to every line in the book (except the signed Appendixes), and we are determined that no wedge should be driven between us. Whether, had we been writing separately, we would all have phrased particular paragraphs as they stand now is not the point; the point is that we are now prepared as individuals to defend the substance of every paragraph. Not that we would go bail for all the opinions we have found in each other in the course of our collaboration. Differences of emphasis and of theological understanding arising from our traditions no doubt remain (often unconsciously). Differences of pastoral practice, ceremonial observances, personal devotion, and other matters persist. We not only have not attempted to iron them out, we would think it unnecessary and perhaps wrong to do so in three months. Catholics and Evangelicals we remain. But above all we are Christians, and we have found our Christianity to run deeper as a common position than we ourselves might well have thought but a year or two ago.

WHAT OF THE FUTURE?

In writing in this way we do not and cannot claim widespread support for our proposals at the point of publication. But our agreements ought to have this value at least—that they take away the last-ditch argument for the last Scheme, that we are disagreed. Others may feel driven to go further and do more. We would dearly love to see this happen. For the moment we can only write as ourselves, owning no man or party as master and being prepared if it is necessary for the misunderstanding of those who have been close to us hitherto. Yet we have good hopes that, despite this risk, the opposite will occur. We look for a widespread discussion that will take our thinking seriously, and the private soundings we have made encourage us to think we shall not look in vain.

We foresee the criticisms to which we shall be open. Why have opponents of the late Scheme worked alone on this? And why have Anglicans worked alone? And why have we not followed the "open-walled" procedures we have ourselves advocated?[1] These questions have obvious force and we feel impelled to answer them. This we do in the reverse order.

We do strongly advocate open-walled procedures still. And we view ourselves as in the middle of them. We have already spoken openly three times[2] before this book is published. Our ideas have not been picked up. The only response has been "tell us more" (or sometimes a cold shoulder). We thus now provide more. But we do not want such a scheme as this to be offered to the Churches for quick decision. That would be hopelessly premature. We need a widespread open-walled discussion to follow our publication. We

[1] See our May Statement, Appendix 1, p. 167.
[2] I.e. the contents of our first three Appendixes.

need others then to contribute. If a consensus about possibilities starts to emerge we shall then need negotiations. We dare not pre-empt any of these processes. We have gone underground for a few months simply because we were told that we could not produce a viable scheme on which we were all agreed, and once it had become clear that we could only do this by setting out a scheme in its entirety we were unwilling to court disaster by piecemeal disclosures of our thinking.

Secondly, we have operated on an Anglican-only basis for reasons compounded of principle and practicability. In principle we have turned our backs on bilateral schemes which postpone further union rather than hasten it.[1] We have thus had no particular reason for including Methodists rather than others, and to do so might have been misunderstood.[2] Once we went beyond Methodism we should not have known where to stop, and the dictates of time precluded leisured round-table conferences such as official bodies might promote. We cannot emphasize too strongly that we are not producing another Anglican–Methodist scheme. And even if we were, geography would have proved a serious practical handicap. It has been basic to our working quickly that we could meet frequently in London, and a more scattered group would have been correspondingly slower in its task. Anglican dissent may not find its best theological expression in the London area—we make no such exclusive claims—but Methodist dissent clearly finds its theological strength in the provinces.

Why then opponents only? Our brief history of recent events should have given the clue to this. We were driven together by the hard line of the proponents of the Scheme. We had no reason to expect openness to dialogue about alternatives until 8 July (at which point no doubt the Bishop of Carlisle and the few like him would have become ready bridges). And by then we had "set" as a group, and we felt it best to remain for the short-term as a closed group. Even our friends have been largely unaware of the directions in which we were proceeding.

Our minds were reinforced in this procedure (rightly or wrongly) by the official continuance of the confrontation. While the late Scheme has been still treated as though it might still have some

---

[1] This point is argued out in Appendix 5, p. 200.
[2] One or two leading Methodist dissentients whom we consulted counselled working on our own, despite their interest and sympathy with the task.

life in it,[1] we have inevitably continued to be cast in the role of opponents. Whereas we had hoped that after 8 July all Christians of goodwill towards the union of the Churches could start again on equal terms, in the event it has not been so. Officialdom has frequently told us that those who favoured the Scheme could never be interested in alternatives,[2] and simultaneously has denounced us for failing to produce widespread support for possible alternatives. Alternatives have become by definition the province, not of the whole of the Church of England (let alone other Churches), as we might have hoped, but solely of those persistent dissentients who are prepared to go the second mile and do the extra work which the logic of their position, as those who desire union but oppose the Scheme, implies.

Nor do we think that this temporary round of small-circle discussion will have done anything but good in the long run. It is in the Church of England if anywhere that the historic differences in Christendom are most dramatically set out in juxtaposition. If in the Church of England the much-vaunted comprehensiveness can be turned actively into the virtue which it has been acclaimed,[3]

---

[1] A characteristic of this has been the "if only" sighing of the majority. "If only 22 proctors had voted the other way, we should have had the 75 % (and perhaps we could still persuade them)." But "if only" has two edges. "If only one Canterbury proctor who voted 'yes' had even abstained, then Canterbury Lower House would not have reached two-thirds", and (as Amos Creswell tellingly said from the floor at Birmingham) "If only 17 members of the Methodist Conference had voted the other way, then Methodism would not have given the Scheme 75 %". To us this seems irrelevant: the ultimate viability of the Scheme never could depend upon how many people got held up at the traffic lights in Westminster or Birmingham and missed the vote! It depends upon the general will of the two bodies. But what is more important is that the *rightness* of a Scheme which involves the substance of the faith cannot be judged on the basis of the presence or absence of a few voters.

[2] Contrary to our expectations, we were each told in 1967 by the Unity Commission that we must not suggest alternatives to them! They viewed their task as solely to make us conform to their Scheme by persuasion.

[3] Much has been made in the past of the comprehensiveness of the Church of England, but too often it has been regarded in too negative and uncreative a way. In the sixteenth century the Church of England found itself for a variety of reasons in the position of having retained much from the past and at the same time having absorbed many aspects of the Reformation. Neither the Catholic looking at its Catholic elements nor the Evangelical looking at its Reformed elements would wish to say that in either respect the Church of England took wholly what was right and good and discarded wholly what was bad. Yet too often this has been the assumption, coupled with regret that the Church of England was not more "Catholic" or more "Reformed" than it was. Too often the wings of the Church of England have been but tolerated, with the implication that the true Anglican was a compromise of moderation. Most of the time the Church of England has

then there could be crystallizing findings of significance for Christendom far beyond the Church of England. Certainly we address our book not only to the Church of England, as though it were an academic exercise in internal adjustments, but to the other Christian Churches in England and beyond, as the sort of thing that the Church of England ought to be able to say to them with one clear voice. If this is understood then further internal dialogue should certainly follow, to see how far the Church of England can adopt this sort of stance, but there should also be external dialogue to see how welcome such a stance would be to others.

If men go on to ask whether those who favoured the late Scheme could well go with this approach we must answer (as the Archbishop said of the Bishop of Ripon on 8 July), "Ask them. They are of age. Let them answer for themselves." We hope that an alternative way forward would at least sort out those who desire the end of union from those who may have become so emotionally involved with the dead Scheme that they cannot detach themselves from it.[1] We are optimistic that much of the support of the Scheme came from those who would in principle accept any viable scheme, but thought that to be the only viable one that could be produced. Now that it has proved not viable and not the only scheme in existence, who would continue to support it through thick and thin?

We have let drop hints above as to the procedures we feel might

presented the spectacle of a rather uneasy federation of groups existing under the umbrella of ambiguous formularies, each group appealing quite legitimately to divines or practices supporting this or that interpretation. Seldom has the peculiar position of the Church of England been seen as providing the opportunity for positive and creative discussion and fellowship between the groups with the one aim of discovering by the guidance of the Holy Spirit what in each tradition witnesses to an essential element of scriptural and catholic truth, what in each tradition is lacking and in what way each tradition, because it has to some degree developed in isolation, has become distorted. Such opportunity should also have extended to consideration of how each element in the Anglican tradition had become unbalanced because of its reactions against the supposed Anglican ideal of moderation in compromise. The existence of the Church of England which, humanly speaking, appears to be due to a historical accident, cannot be justified by appeals to a national basis, any more than the Anglican Communion can be justified by appealing to the political Commonwealth. It can only be justified if the opportunity given within it for creative thought and action in obedience to revealed truth is seized with both hands.

[1] It has thus been saddening to hear the President-designate of the Methodist Conference say in public that if an alternative is produced the Methodist Church does not want it, as she is committed to the late Scheme and not prepared to retrace any steps.

be followed if the contents of this book win any public interest. It may be best here simply to repeat that initially any discussion ought no more to be concerned with how to implement this scheme than with how to implement the old one. Discussion must restart with the broadest terms of reference, for the right people to find, by the deepest exploration of theology and the widest exploration of what is viable, just how to unite the people of God in this country. Lord Fisher set the direction for twenty-three years by a single sermon. It has proved a cul-de-sac. We have no wish to subject the Church to the same experience through a single book, however thoroughgoing the debate of the four men who produced it.

We might go further. There is a real distinction to be drawn between finding a viable scheme for union and setting a time-table for implementation. We have addressed ourselves solely to the former of these tasks. We are not only not urging that a scheme of union ought to be implemented by a fixed date (e.g. Easter 1980). On the contrary we are urging that no date should be fixed. It is the sense that time is running out that produces unprincipled pressures for the implementation of particular schemes. Nevertheless we believe that the actual scheme we offer, or some variant embodying the same principles, would in fact bring true organic union far in advance of any prospect it had under the late Scheme.

THE SHAPE OF THE BOOK

We have attempted to group all our forward-looking thinking into a logical order as the main fourteen chapters of the book. The imagery of the temple in Eph. 2. 19–22 has never been far from us, and the section headings give expression to this. We are not so earthbound, we hope, as to imagine that mere ecclesiastical joinery can be called God's joining of the structure. But we consider that a union implemented in the way we suggest would be a good instrument for the hand of God the master-builder. Without his Spirit their labour is but vain who build.

Some backward-looking material and one or two other things have been reserved for Appendixes. The first two are self-explanatory. The third was the first step in building together, and we feel deserves to be reprinted to take its place with the rest. The fourth deals with a subject vital to a *rapprochement* of Catholics and Evangelicals but perhaps not quite so obviously vital to a scheme of union. It enables Michael Green to continue his association with a group in which he had a formative hand, and it brings together two theologians who had previously been orientated over against each other. These four Appendixes are signed, whereas the next three spring from the main group of four authors, and do some necessary clearing up of the past and keeping the record straight.

We have hesitated to ascribe our doings to the Spirit of God. Only time will tell how far this is his work, and how far a passing human endeavour. But we know that if there is treasure here it is in earthen vessels. We have had no time for smoothing disparate styles, invoking recondite works of reference, compiling lengthy indexes. The transition from one chapter to another is often rough and abrupt. There are repetitions and overlaps. We know it ourselves. But time would not wait for us, and so we have done simply what we could. There is scriptural precedent.

COLIN BUCHANAN

E. L. MASCALL

J. I. PACKER

✠GRAHAM WILLESDEN

8 January 1970

PART ONE

Foundation and Cornerstone

"You are...built upon the foundation of the apostles and pro-
phets, Jesus Christ himself being the chief cornerstone."
Ephesians 2. 20

This first part of the book takes up fundamental questions of
theology, particularly those over which Catholics and Evangelicals
have hitherto been prone to disagree. Their aim is to stake out firm
ground for the later building, and to lay the foundations properly
on it. The agreements registered here have a significance over and
above the question of whether the scheme we provide is viable or
not, but equally the scheme itself is wholly dependent upon them.
We cannot build without foundations.

1

Scripture and Tradition

The question of Scripture and Tradition is one which has consciously divided the Churches of the Reformation from the Church of Rome since the sixteenth century, and Anglicans from Anglicans since the commencement of the Catholic Revival in the 1830s. It is in fact a quite fundamental question, for our view both of the doctrinal and ethical content of Christian faith as a whole, and of the way to determine and delimit that content when controversies arise, will depend directly on our understanding of what Scripture and Tradition are, and how they stand related. Our method of theological construction, our practice of biblical interpretation, and our view of the Christian principle of authority, all turn on how we resolve this basic issue.

In recent years much rethinking of this question has taken place, and it is clear that definite progress has been made in removing misunderstandings and clarifying alternative positions; though it is equally clear that not all the differences have yet been resolved. Hence it is important for us to face this issue squarely at the start of our own book. The spectacle of a group of Catholic and Evangelical Anglicans testifying to what they believe to be important agreements (and this is the spectacle which we present) will naturally prompt readers to wonder how deep these agreements really go—whether they indicate genuine and abiding correspondence of theological outlook and method, or whether they are merely transient phenomena, born of a particular phase of domestic debate and likely to perish with it. What long-term significance might attach to our present conjunction? Could it be a growing-point for the future? Neither we ourselves, nor our readers, can know unless we address ourselves directly to the problem of Scripture and Tradition, and explore together the question how the authoritative truth which the Church must obey is to be known.

It will be salutary, if chastening, for us to start by noting the stereotypes of our positions which have long been current in the

Church of England. Historically, both Evangelicals and Catholics have seen each other as involved, by reason of a faulty approach to the Scripture–Tradition problem, in a faulty grasp of the deposit of faith and a faulty mode of interpreting the Bible itself. Evangelicals have seen Catholic convictions concerning the necessity of bishops in apostolic succession, the sacramental significance of confirmation and confession, the eucharistic presence and sacrifice, and the uncertain ecclesial status of the Free Churches, as directly due to an improper use of Tradition as a second source of doctrine, over and above the Scriptures (which, it has been argued, will not themselves justify any of these disputed positions). Catholics have in the past seen Evangelical counter-convictions on these points, together with what has seemed to them an intolerably "low" view of the visible Church and an impossibly individualistic understanding of the Christian life, as directly due to an improper use of the Bible which has isolated it from its true context in the Church's continuing life, the context in which alone it can be rightly understood, and has pressed it into the service of unbiblical negations. Thus each side has accused the other of muzzling the word of God. Evangelicals have argued that on Catholic principles, which yoke the Bible to tradition, Scripture cannot reform the Church when it goes wrong; the Catholic reply has been that on Evangelical principles, which set the Bible against Tradition, Scripture cannot form the Church in the way that is right. This is the issue between conservative Catholics and Evangelicals as it is commonly understood.

IS TRADITION A "SECOND SOURCE"?

We wish, however, as the first step in our own discussion, to question the assumption about tradition which appears to underlie this view of the case—namely, the assumption that Tradition is a second source of doctrine, distinct from the Bible.

In his book, *Holy Writ or Holy Church*, Father Tavard has forcefully argued that this is an assumption originating in the late Middle Ages. He maintains that the notion of Scripture and Tradition as two parallel and virtually unconnected sources of Christian doctrine can be traced back only to the fourteenth century and that before that time, as in the early Church, they were conceived in a more flexible and dynamic way and as having an organic connection with each other. (It is noteworthy that in the writings of

St Thomas Aquinas *Sacra Scriptura* frequently denotes the whole body of the Church's dogmatic teaching.) In the sixteenth century most Catholics and Protestants appear to have accepted the theological adequacy of the two-source formula, and of the diagnosis that Catholics accepted both sources and Protestants only one. Nevertheless, vestiges of the earlier view remained. The Council of Trent did not commit itself to the two-source formula and, while affirming that Christian truth is to be found in both written Scripture and unwritten apostolic Tradition, ignored the statement of an earlier draft that it is to be found partly in the one and partly in the other; it is thus open to a Roman Catholic (though until quite recently few have done this) to be loyal to Trent and yet hold that, whatever part Tradition may play in its preservation and formulation, all Christian truth is to be found in Scripture. We may also remark that Trent explicitly says that "the source" (*fontem*, in the singular) of Christian truth as regards both faith and morals is in fact "the Gospel" preached first by Jesus with his own mouth and then committed to his Apostles. Vatican II, in its decree on Revelation, while endorsing the Tridentine teaching, very significantly takes as its starting-point the revelation given by God in Christ; Tradition and Scripture are in close connection and communication with each other, since both flow from the same "divine wellspring" (*scaturigo*). We shall return to this in a moment.

The view of tradition as a separate source of truth, distinct from the Bible, was buttressed for centuries by the extremely static view of Christian doctrine which was common to all parties in the Reformation and post-Reformation period. Dr Owen Chadwick has highlighted this in his book *From Bossuet to Newman*. Not only in substance but in minute detail both Protestants and Catholics were anxious to prove that what they said and did was exactly what was said and done by the Apostles and the Fathers; any conception of development of doctrine was to all intents and purposes absent until the time of Newman. Now we are as anxious as anyone to insist that Jesus Christ is the full and final revelation of God; in him dwells all the fullness of the Godhead bodily and he alone is the Saviour of mankind. Nevertheless there can be and is development in the Church's understanding of the Gospel, and it is a legitimate criticism of a great deal of post-Reformation theology, both Catholic and Protestant, that it has tended to interpret both the Scriptures and the other documents of the Church in a very wooden way without reference to their history and their context. Not only did this tendency prevent the recovery of a dynamic view of Tradition as essentially the process of the handing on by the Church of the faith of the Scriptures; it also enthroned the static view, which first reduced tradition to a series of traditions, and then represented these as units of divine truth having their status independent of the Bible.

TWO FURTHER MODERN DISTORTIONS

Two further points must be noted at this stage. First, on the Protestant side, the historic appeal to Scripture has in recent years been seriously undermined in many quarters by the impact of biblical scholarship, especially that of the form-critical school. Much of this writing seems to us to be highly speculative and questionable but its effects are undeniable. When, for example, we see Dr Kurt Aland[1] seeking a "canon within the canon" as the only authentic element in Scripture, or Dr Nygren[2] detecting a declension from the purity of the Gospel in the Johannine books themselves, or Dr Käsemann[3] asserting that the Fourth Gospel is a gnostic work which radically distorts both the teaching and the significance of Jesus, we can hardly fail to be conscious of the destructive effect of this type of scholarship on the authority of the Scriptures in Protestantism. If the New Testament is now to be downgraded as unauthentic, just as unwritten traditions were downgraded by the first Protestants four centuries ago, the question of the relation between Scripture and Tradition becomes a trivial one, on which nothing decisive hinges—the only question then is, which of these historico-critical popes we should trust to tell us, on the basis of his scholarly speculations, what the substance of Christianity really is.

Secondly, on the Catholic side, as Dr J. P. Mackey has shown in *The Modern Doctrine of Tradition*, there has been during the past hundred years a very strong tendency to assimilate tradition to the contemporary *magisterium* of the Church. This is in practice equivalent to ignoring tradition, in the historical sense, altogether, since if I can ascertain the truth by consulting the contemporary authorities what need can there be to investigate the past? Pius IX's famous remark, "La tradizione son' io", may not be authentic

[1] *The Problem of the New Testament Canon.*
[2] *Agape and Eros.*   [3] *Commentary on the Fourth Gospel.*

but it expresses the attitude admirably. More recently, however, responsible Roman Catholic theologians have emphasized that a certain character of relativity attaches to even the most august deliverances of authority, and that these must always be situated in the historical context from which they emerged if their significance is to be properly understood. It is not, on this view, that Pius IX speaking *ex cathedra* is not Tradition, but that there is always far more to Tradition than Pius IX speaking *ex cathedra*. In some Roman Catholic circles this emphasis has resulted in a complete rejection of the notion of authority in the Church, parallel to the rejection by liberal Protestantism of the notion of authority in relation to the Bible; in more responsible hands, however, it implies a very salutary use of tradition, in the sense of the specific witness of Church authorities on specific issues, at specific times, in the past, as a check upon contemporary divagations of the *magisterium*. If Vatican II is serious in its assertion *Ecclesia semper reformanda*, Tradition in this sense, as well as Scripture, will have its part to play in the needed reformation. Certainly, the full historical dimensions of Tradition, as the Church's transmission of the faith down the ages, must be preserved in our thinking, if the true shape of the Scripture–Tradition problem is to be seen.

The purpose of the above paragraphs has been to pave the way for the statement of our own main theme, placing it in its own contemporary setting. That theme is this: *the ground of both Scripture and Tradition, the reality to which both point, is the fact of divine Revelation given fully and finally in and through Jesus Christ, who is both the Word and the Wisdom of the Father and who, by his crucifixion and resurrection, has redeemed the human race.* We recognize the partial and progressive revelation given to the Jewish people under the old dispensation; we affirm that it has found its fulfilment and culmination in Christ, who both climaxes and terminates it. It is not our purpose here to call in question whether, in a secondary sense, the term "revelation" may be properly given to the knowledge of himself which God has given through the non-Christian religions and through his work in creation (Acts 14. 17; Rom. 1. 20), or whether, in a further secondary sense, it may properly be applied to the Bible itself, in which this revelation is authoritatively recorded. Both usages are, of course, ancient, and our argument does not require us to controvert them. What we are concerned to maintain is that salvation, the reconciliation of man to God, wherever and whenever it is attained, derives from God's decision to reveal *himself*, and to do so in Jesus Christ who is both God and man.

CHRIST AND REVELATION

The fact that God's full and final revelation is given in a person is of the utmost significance. It has often been asserted in recent years that God reveals himself in acts and not in words, and some have rightly taken up the cudgels to vindicate the place of words in the revelatory process; the deeper truth is, however, that because we who are to be redeemed are persons, God has revealed himself to us in a person and as a person, and both his acts and his words ultimately derive from this. The part played by words in revelation should not be belittled; speech—the ability to communicate by words—is one of the gifts that distinguish man from the lower creation, and the Saviour himself was the Rabbi, the Teacher, who taught by words as well as by deeds. How, in any case, can we describe God's acts themselves except by words? And how could we know their meaning and place in his plan without words from God to instruct us? How, for instance, could anyone have *guessed* that the sordid liquidating of an off-beat religious teacher in an obscure Roman province was the redemption of the world, if God had not spoken to tell us so? Nevertheless, the fact remains that the central and basic locus of God's full and final revelation was neither impersonal acts nor verbal statements as such, but a Person, and all God's dealings with man must be seen in relation to him. Therefore, both Scripture and Tradition must be seen as deriving from Christ and as confronting men with him. Our understanding of them, as of everything else in the Christian religion, must be Christological; and because the Church is the Body of Christ, it must be ecclesiological.

The real defect of the two-source view was that it looked upon Scripture and Tradition as two parallel entities, each having the same essentially verbal nature. Written Scripture and non-written Tradition (or traditions) were both conceived as consisting of so many holy words. Tradition, however, as the early Church thought of it, is something much wider and more living than this. As *traditio—paradosis*—it is the handing on to each Christian of the riches of the Father's house to which he became entitled by his baptism; as *traditum* it is the riches themselves which are handed

34

on. And Scripture is included in these riches. In the Church's very earliest days, the Scriptures handed on were simply the Jewish Scriptures, those which we call the Old Testament, which, following Christ's own teaching, were taken as prophetic of Christ and as fulfilled in him, and were therefore claimed by the Church as divine instruction which had had Christians in view all along. Even in the later Nicene Creed, when we are told that Christ rose from the dead "according to the Scriptures", the meaning is not that he rose as the New Testament asserts (though that is perfectly true) but that he rose as the Old Testament foretold. Some of the Fathers contrast Judaism as the religion of a Book with Christianity as the religion of a living and glorified personal Saviour; the Old Testament was not seen as fulfilled in the New Testament (which as a collected corpus had not yet come into existence) but as fulfilled in Christ.

CHURCH AND SCRIPTURE

Nevertheless, when the early material concerning the acts and words of Christ was assembled into the form of our Gospels and when the other books that now form the New Testament came into circulation, all proceeding from the circle of authoritative inspiration which had the Apostles at its centre, it was natural and right that their authority should be recognized, and it was under the providence of God that this took place. It is truer to say that the New Testament canon established itself by consensus than that it was established at any stage by formal legislation; it seems certain, however, that the canonical status of most of the books, and certainly most of the major books, of the New Testament was effectively recognized throughout the Church before the end of the second century, as a result of reflection and inquiry provoked by the production of Marcion's truncated canon, on the one hand, and, on the other hand, by the discovery that spurious books bearing apostolic names had begun to circulate. The Church did not believe itself to be conferring authority upon any of the books by recognizing them as authoritative; their authority was assumed without question to be intrinsic, deriving from the Christ who had bestowed the charisma of inspiration upon the circle of witnesses to which their authors had belonged. In the sense that the churches were testing the claims of various books to be authentically apostolic in origin and content, it may be truly said that the Church was sitting in judgement on the Scriptures in deciding the canon; but it must also be said at once that the Church was only doing this in order that the Scriptures should sit in judgement upon the Church. But the whole notion of sitting in judgement is really inappropriate in any case when the reality of the situation was that God was guiding his Church by his Spirit to recognize the Scriptures which he had given it.

We have spoken of Scripture as divinely inspired—*theopneustos*, "breathed out by God". There are many problems about biblical inspiration which have not been adequately discussed or satisfactorily determined; like all problems involving the relation between divine and human activity, they are extremely difficult, and they need much more attention than they have yet received. This much, however, is certain: that the effect of inspiration was to produce a presentation and interpretation of the revelatory and redemptive fact of Christ that is normative for the Church's faith and life for all time.

Professor R. P. C. Hanson, in his book *Tradition in the Early Church*, has pointed out that in the earliest period when the scriptural canon was as yet undetermined and some of the books were not universally known, Tradition held a larger place than Scripture in the preservation and propagation of the Church's entire faith, whereas later on the situation tended to be reversed. This is only natural. The supreme importance of Scripture as the normative element in the Church's tradition arises from its character as, so to speak, the verbal precipitate of the Church's primordial life and, therefore, as keeping the Church true to its historical roots as nothing else, except perhaps the Eucharist, can. This is true even when we recognize a development of doctrinal understanding within the New Testament itself; even those who seek for a canon within the canon or a gospel behind the Gospels have to go to the canon and the Gospels for their material. The Scriptures would have this supreme importance even if they were purely human compositions accidentally assembled, but their importance is enhanced yet further when we see the gracious hand of God at work both in the production of the Scriptures and in his gift of them to the Church.

TOWARDS A RESOLUTION

Scripture and Tradition, then, belong together. They are diverse in character but are organically related in accordance with their several natures. The activity of tradition (the handing-on process) is one essential form of the Church's ongoing life. The content of tradition (that which is handed on) is, in idea and intention at any rate, precisely the faith of the Scriptures. Tradition cut off from Scripture is likely to become undisciplined and unbalanced, and even positively distorted; on the other hand, Scripture cut off from the living tradition of the Church can come to seem remote and irrelevant. It is in the fellowship of faith of the Christian community that the Bible will most fully come to life. And neither Scripture nor Tradition can fulfil its true function in the Body of Christ unless both are viewed and understood in living relation to Christ, who is the personal Revelation of God. This is the truth that underlies the emphasis which Protestantism lays on the preaching of the word of God and which Catholicism lays upon the administration of the sacraments. For both preacher and celebrant are commissioned as personal agents through whom the personal Christ makes himself personally known to personal human beings. The function of either is gravely misconceived if this is ever forgotten. So Scripture, under Christ, should be thought of as the normative element in Tradition; and Tradition, under Christ, should be thought of as the vitalizing *milieu* of Scripture. Neither, however, can be its true self if it is cut off from the living Christ and from the Spirit of Christ who guides and illuminates and re-forms Christ's Body, the Church.

This is simply to say that what the traditionary process passes on should be viewed in the first instance as a primary and provisional exposition of the biblical faith, and that what is written in the biblical documents should be viewed in the first instance as the archetypal and normative tradition, the authentic apostolic *paradosis* which must both form and, where necessary, reform the later *paradosis* in order that the knowledge of Christ should not be obscured. Ecclesiastical tradition exists because of the work of the Spirit, for it is the precipitate of the understanding which the Spirit has given and deepened down the ages of what the apostolic witness to Christ means and implies, and how it may find expression. The Holy Scriptures also exist because of the work of the

37

Spirit, who, having led the early Church to receive the Old Testament as divine instruction for Christians, caused the apostolic witness to be written down and then recognized as authoritative, alongside the Old Testament, in its written form. Tradition, however venerable, is not infallible as a mode of transmission, and needs constantly to be tested by the Scriptures whose witness to Christ it seeks to convey. Scripture, however inspired, was not meant to be self-sufficient as a means of instruction and life, but to operate within the common life of the Christian community by way of preaching, sacrament, fellowship, and prayers. Reformation Protestantism, arguing against the idea of an ecclesiastical *magisterium* acting as a second source of doctrine and an infallible interpreter of Scripture, rightly maintained that Scripture was *clear* in its meaning and *sufficient* in its content for purposes of salvation, and that the *magisterium* affirmed by Rome was superfluous; yet the fact remains that the witness of Scripture to Christ will be made clearer, and its contents come to be better known and appreciated, within the living fellowship of the people of God, as Catholic eucharistic experience and Evangelical group Bible study alike proclaim. Scripture and Tradition are thus from every standpoint not antithetical, but complementary as means of leading us to Christ.

A POINT OF DEPARTURE

Once this is accepted, the ground is clear for the theological endeavour of this present book. As long as Catholics see Evangelicals as bogged down in a biblicism which refuses to contemplate theological justification for formulations and institutions not exemplified in the Scriptures, or to entertain exegetical hypotheses which posit as the background of biblical statements factors which only later worked their way into explicit historical expression, and as long as Evangelicals see Catholics as trapped in a traditionalism which refuses to face requests for scriptural justification of elements in tradition, or to allow that what cannot be so justified may not be put forward as a universal norm, little can be done together in dealing with the matters of conventional dispute; the only course open then would be to see if we can agree to differ, on the ground that none of these matters of disputes is of much importance (which is, in effect, what the rejected Anglican–Methodist Scheme was asking us to do). But the argument we have pursued has already led us beyond this point of blockage. By allowing that the content of the traditionary process and the scriptural documents is ideally coincident, we have committed ourselves on the one hand to take with full seriousness any theological justification of traditional positions and institutions that may be offered on the basis of the biblical witness to the living Christ and his Church, and we have committed ourselves on the other hand to take with equal seriousness any plea for such justification, or complaint of lack of it, that may be pressed upon us. It is by dialogue along these lines that the agreements set forth in this book have been hammered out.

2

God and his Grace

THEISM

"In the beginning, God created": so begins the Bible, and so begins all sound theology. The Creator–creature distinction is a basic frame of reference apart from which thoughts about God cannot be true. Therefore when Paul, the Christian theist, went to polytheistic Athens, and was asked to give the Athenian public an account of his message, he did not introduce Jesus and the resurrection at the outset (these themes came later), but started with that which is the presupposition for understanding both—namely, the reality, activity, and claims of God the Creator. Ignorance of his reality, activity, and claims (so Paul affirmed) had made him a God unknown to the Athenians.

> What you worship but do not know—this is what I now proclaim.
> The God who created the world and everything in it, and who is Lord of heaven and earth...is himself the universal giver of life and breath and all else. He created every race of men of one stock, to inhabit the whole earth's surface. He fixed the epochs of their history and the limits of their territory (Acts 17. 23–6, N.E.B.).

This God—omnipotent, independent, eternal, the God of the Bible and the God of the gospel—is a God to be confessed and a God to be worshipped. "Of him, and through him, and to him, are all things: to whom be glory for ever. Amen" (Rom. 11. 36). "Source, Guide, and Goal of all that is" is how the N.E.B. renders the opening sentence of this doxology. Spinoza has been called "God-intoxicated" for his pantheism; how much more does the description fit Paul, with his Christian theism!

In face of the unbalanced immanentism of modern theology, Paul's point still has to be made time and time again. "The God and Father of our Lord Jesus Christ" is more than a cosmic function or value, a dimension of depth or challenge in men and things. He is the transcendent Creator on whom men and things depend for their being from moment to moment. The very power to misconceive and deny him is his gift to us. A further reference to Christian worship is the quickest and most telling way to make the point. The facts of worship are here more significant than the history of debates; for Christians are at their maddest in argument, and at their sanest in worship. What, we ask, has been going on in Christian worship over the past nineteen centuries? Why, just this: Christians have together been bowing down before an omnipotent personal Creator, a living, speaking God who addresses and draws near to men by means of his Word and sacraments, and to whom they draw near in response through praise and prayer. This has been true in every type and tradition of Christianity. And what has been the main theme of their worship, the burden of their eucharists and baptisms, of the Bible they read and the gospel they preached, of their prayers and hymns and thanksgivings? Again, one answer can be given for all. The theme of Christian worship is, and always has been, God's *saving grace*.

JUSTIFICATION

It is a commonplace that nothing like the Bible idea of grace— free, unmerited, unsolicited love, taking the initiative to rescue the undeserving and enrich the unlovely—has ever been known in any other religion. It is not always seen that this is a direct consequence of the uniqueness of biblical theism. Only a personal God can love to the uttermost; only an omnipotent God can save to the uttermost. Catholic and Evangelical alike have traditionally shown a true instinct in seeing Pelagianism, the doctrine of self-salvation through self-sufficient self-reliance, as among the profoundest of heresies. Where Pelagianism is, the true recognition and valuation of saving grace is not, and this lack tears out the very heart of worship.

The most massive expositions of God's sovereign saving grace that the New Testament contains are found in the writings of the Apostle Paul, and the central concept in Paul's account of saving grace is the concept of God's act of justifying the ungodly (Paul's phrase, Rom. 4. 5)—that is, constituting them righteous and accepted in his sight here and now. It has been questioned whether justification was to Paul anything more than a controversial device developed for *ad hominem* use against the Jews. When, however, one weighs the fact that the Epistle to the Romans is in intention a full-dress exposition of the gospel, and justification ("the righteousness of God") is its main theme; plus the fact that when Paul opens his heart to speak of his personal faith, he does it regularly in justification terms (Gal. 2. 15–21; 2 Cor. 5. 16–21; Phil. 3. 4–14); plus the further fact that God's justifying purpose is the main theme of Paul's philosophy of church and world history (Gal. 3; Rom. 9–11); plus the fact also that for Paul justification is a basic and far-reaching blessing, at once righting the past and securing the future (Rom. 5. 1–10); plus the final fact that justification (the forgiveness of sins together with the gift of peace) is directly correlative to the cross in which Paul glories (Rom. 3. 24; Gal. 3. 13; etc.)—then it becomes clear that justification is right at the heart of Paul's understanding of grace. The Dutch divine G. C. Berkouwer speaks for Paul, as well as for the Reformed tradition out of which he writes, when he declares: "The confession of divine justification touches man's life at its heart, at the point of its relationship to God; it defines the preaching of the church, the existence and progress of the life of faith, the root of human security, and man's perspective for the future."[1] The doctrine of justification is, in truth, of the essence of the gospel.

THE SIXTEENTH-CENTURY DIVIDE

But by mentioning the Reformed tradition we have reminded ourselves of the shadow that hangs over any discussion of this subject—namely, the fact that since the sixteenth century the doctrine of justification has been a storm-centre in Christendom, as being a central issue in the Reformation protest. Lutherans have often called justification by faith the material principle of the Reformation, along with the appeal to Scripture as its formal principle. All discussions of justification for the past four centuries have taken place under the shadow of the Reformation division, with the result that expositors have taken their cue from sixteenth-century debates and accustomed themselves to state the doctrine antithetically, offsetting it from the supposed misunderstanding of it on the other side. This has been no less true of Evangelical and Catholic Anglicans than of Protestants and Roman Catholics generally. Thus, Anglican Evangelicals have accused Anglican

---

[1] *Faith and Justification* (Grand Rapids), p. 17.

Catholics of corporate legalism, and Catholic Anglicans have accused Evangelical Anglicans of individualistic antinomianism, each on the ground that the other has failed to grasp the real meaning of justification. Yet when all parties to these debates profess to oppose Pelagianism and to be concerned to magnify God's free and sovereign grace, it is hard to believe that the differences about justification are irreconcilable. Indeed, there has been a striking ecumenical *rapprochement* on the subject during the past generation, as the following review will show.

In the sixteenth century official Protestantism, as represented by its confessions and theological leaders, and official Romanism, as represented by the Council of Trent and defenders of Trent like Bellarmine, polarized over six issues in the doctrine of justification. They were as follows:

First, the question of how justification and sanctification were related. Rome held (see Trent) that God's declaration of acceptance and remission of sins rests upon the first act of sanctification through baptismal grace, and insisted, against New Testament lexicography (as scholars pointed out in the sixteenth century, and point out still), that the concept of justification includes both the initial subjective renewal and the consequent divine declaration.

Second, whether the "formal cause" of justification (i.e. that which gives us the righteous quality which God's justifying sentence declares us to have) is Christ's righteousness imputed or God's righteousness imparted. Trent said the latter, Protestants generally said the former; the question was much debated in the late sixteenth and seventeenth centuries.

Third, whether the "concupiscence" that remains in the baptized person has the nature of sin, rendering one guilty in God's sight, or whether the baptized person, despite his indwelling "concupiscence", may properly be regarded as perfect and meritorious before God. Protestants, following Augustine, took the former line; Rome, the latter.

Fourth, whether "implicit faith" (an intention of believing what the Church believes, which Rome judges sufficient for the sacraments) will save, or whether there is not need of fiducial faith (faith that involves application of the good news of grace to oneself in active trust towards Christ, and so has in it a dimension of assurance). Rome said the former, Protestants the latter.

Fifth, whether an offering of Christ and his sacrifice to God by the priest in the Eucharist is part of God's revealed plan for the putting away of sins. Two issues were, of course, involved here: the nature of the Eucharist, and the priesthood of the minister. Rome affirmed the Mass, Protestants vehemently rejected it.

Sixth, whether the concepts of fiducial faith, imputed righteousness, and declarative justification, taken together, do not imply a salvation of which subjective righteousness and holy living are not integral parts. Rome pressed this against the Protestants, who vehemently denied that their position on these matters carried with it any such inference.

At the time of the Catholic Revival in England, debate on a number of these issues broke out afresh among Anglicans. Newman's *Lectures on Justification*, which sought to synthesize Roman and Protestant elements, purifying both, but leaned heavily in the Roman direction; plus general Tractarian animosity to "Lutheran solifidianism", as being antinomian; plus a polemical emphasis, against Evangelicals, on the cruciality of sanctification, the need for imparted righteousness, baptismal regeneration, sacramental confession as the ordinary means of having one's sins forgiven, and the prerogatives of the institutional Church in this matter—all contributed to the general view (sometimes still found, though without much real evidence to back it up) that Anglican Catholics had simply lined up on the Roman side.

THE TWENTIETH-CENTURY RAPPROCHEMENT

So the traditional lines of debate were drawn. But in recent years three factors have put new life into the discussion of justification, and led, as it appears, to positive ecumenical advance.

In the first place, the revival of biblical theology throughout the Church has produced a wide consensus that

(*a*) justification in the New Testament belongs to a basically forensic model of man's relations with God, into which, speaking purely conceptually, sanctification does not enter;[1]

(*b*) God's justifying act belongs to a total salvation "in Christ", of which subjective renewal is an integral part;

---

[1] The Roman divine Hans Küng brings this out very strongly in his Excursus "Justification and Sanctification according to the New Testament" in *Justification* (London 1964), pp. 289 ff.

(c) Christ's unique priesthood is all-sufficient, and his priestly ministry is that on which our salvation directly depends;

(d) the fiducial element is essential to faith in God and in Christ.

Then, in the second place, the twentieth-century revival of Reformation study has shown that Luther and those who followed him did not separate justification from sanctification ontologically. The idea that Luther believed there was no subjective change at all in the man whom God declares and calls righteous is groundless. Writers like Louis Bouyer, in *The Spirit and Forms of Protestantism*, have supposed that Luther's formula for the state of the justified man, *simul justus et peccator* ("at the same time a righteous man and a sinner"), and his habitual insistence on the reality of sin and non-merit in the Christian, obliging him to cling to Christ for pardon every moment, indicated a nominalist quality in his thinking about the Christian life which excluded all thought of a real sanctification. But Luther's nominalism, as scholars are seeing with increasing clarity, was only skin-deep. Certainly, his stress on good works as the inseparable concomitants of a living faith makes the idea that he did not believe that justification was accompanied by a subjective change look rather absurd.

Finally, in the third place, Hans Küng has shown that when verbal differences are taken account of, the teaching of the Council of Trent and Karl Barth on justification can be substantially brought into line. Questions still remain: it has to be asked, for instance, whether Küng is fair to Trent in ignoring the organic link which it posits between justification and the sacraments of the Church, or between faith and the tradition of the Church, and it also has to be asked whether Küng is entitled to assume that Barth's Christ and covenant of grace can be identified with the Christ and covenant of grace which we meet in the Reformers. But, even if the answer to both questions proves to be "no", Küng's book has undoubtedly opened a new era of discussion and dialogue on justification, and this is no mean achievement.

AGREEMENTS ON GRACE

The old polemical way of Catholic–Evangelical discussion of anything was based on asking at the start how much the parties needed to say against each other. The better way (as we think) is to start by seeing how much they can say together. This is the way that our present book seeks to follow. At no point do we suggest that no further problems or disagreements remain, but all along we are immensely heartened by the extent to which we can claim to stand on common ground. Regarding grace and justification in particular, having surveyed the Reformation cleavage and noted how in modern discussion the gaps are starting to narrow, we now propose to set out eight theses of our own, which we believe show significant agreement on the major issues.

(1) *Grace is the Triune God loving men.* Divine grace is personal, sovereign, and free. It is personal, because God is personal, in the mystery of his eternal and essential tripersonality. It is sovereign, because God is Creator, and the Creator is Lord of his world. It is free, because it flows spontaneously and gratuitously from God himself, and is not called forth by anything attractive in man. Man, indeed, merits divine rejection for his sins; but grace is God's mercy triumphing over his just wrath. Grace is not personal without being sovereign (that would argue divine impotence), nor sovereign without being personal (that would argue an ultimate fatalism), nor is it free in the sense of being arbitrary (that would turn grace into caprice divorced from character). But grace is the action of a God who does not need us, loving us steadfastly in face of all the guilt, uncleanness, and alienation that he sees in us, and saving us victoriously from sin and evil, at whatever cost to himself.

(2) *Grace in this fallen world is the Triune God enriching sinners in and through Jesus Christ.* "Grace and truth came by Jesus Christ" (John 1. 17). Jesus the Christ is God the Son, who became man and was crucified, and is now risen, ascended, enthroned, and coming again. He, as the God-man, is our prophet, priest, and king. Grace, one might say, *is* Jesus Christ, in the sense that he is at once the token of God's love and the means of our benefiting by it. "There is one mediator between God and men, the man Christ Jesus, who gave himself a ransom for all" (1 Tim. 2. 5–6). The incarnation is the *central* Christian fact, no doubt, since it contains in itself the possibility of the redemption of our whole manhood, or, to put it another way, the possibility of our fallen and vitiated humanity becoming as fully human as was Christ's; but the cross and resurrection are the *decisive* Christian facts, as actually securing redemption and new life for us through Christ's atoning achievement in our place.

"Christ hath redeemed us from the curse of the law"—how?—
"being made a curse for us" (Gal. 3. 13). Christ "was delivered for
our offences, and was raised again for our justification" (Rom. 4. 25).
"If Christ be not raised, your faith is vain; ye are yet in your sins"
(1 Cor. 15. 17). "In baptism also you were raised to life with him
through your faith in the active power of God who raised him
from the dead. And although you were dead because of your sins . . .
he has made you alive with Christ. For he has forgiven us all our
sins" (Col. 2. 12–14, N.E.B.). To make the point that the Christian
community shares a new humanity in Christ, some have spoken of
the Church as an extension of the incarnation; but a more biblical
way of making this point would be to speak of the Church as an
extension of the resurrection.

(3) *God's way in grace requires of us total dependence on God in
Jesus Christ for our salvation.* "There is none other name given
under heaven among men, whereby we must be saved" (Acts 4. 12).
Pelagianism in doctrine, and self-reliance in practice, must be our
constant foes. Specifically, we must acknowledge our total dependence on the priestly work of Christ (his once-for-all sacrifice, and
his heavenly intercession) for our forgiveness, present access to
God, and hope of future glory. We may not wholly agree in our
understanding of the atoning event and Christ's heavenly ministry;
we may not all lay the same emphasis on the penal and substitu-
tionary character of our Lord's representative suffering on the cross,
or on the thought that Christ's presence in heaven, as such, on our
behalf, constitutes the essence of his intercession (though none of
us would deny either assertion as true in its place); nonetheless,
these differences of emphasis seem to us secondary, and the fact of
primary importance appears to us to be our agreement regarding
the need for total dependence on Christ's priestly work, first on the
cross and now from the throne.

(4) *Justification is God's acceptance of sinners through Jesus Christ,
and in Jesus Christ, into a new life of forgiveness, communion, and
hope.* Justification is correlative to the cross, the completion of the
great exchange whereby God the Father "made him to be sin for
us, who knew no sin; that we might be made the righteousness of
God in him" (2 Cor. 5. 21). The forensic thought-model of God as
lawgiver and judge, of sin as lawlessness and transgression, of God's
judicial wrath against sinners being quenched by sacrifice, and of
justification as a paradoxical acquittal and acceptance of the ungodly

before God's judgement-seat, permeates the Bible and must be taken as one basic and normative category, not capable of reduction to, or explanation in terms of, any other. Not that it is the only thought-model of which this is true: the organic incorporation-model of our Lord as the last Adam, the vine in which we are branches, the head of the body of which we are members, is equally ultimate, and in fact a true doctrine of justification is only achieved when set in the context of incorporation. For it is only in Christ that any part of our salvation is enjoyed, and in Christ all the various aspects of it are enjoyed together, as indeed our next thesis declares.

(5) *The divine act of grace in which the declaration that a believing sinner is justified is central and basic is in its totality an act of effective and vital union with the living Christ, and hence is constitutive of a new creation.* Thus it can truly be said that God's justifying word (which is a creative word, effecting union with Christ) creates subjective righteousness; though it must always be emphasized that the word of acquittal and acceptance is pronounced on the basis of Christ's vicarious obedience and suffering for us, not on the basis of any aspect of the new creation itself. This is simply to say that justification through Christ, and regeneration in Christ, belong and are given together; the new status and the new life are complementary and inseparable aspects of what it means to be in Christ. Thus it is ontologically impossible that a man whom God has justified should not also be a man who is united to Christ by the indwelling Holy Spirit, and consequently a man in whom the fruits of new life are appearing. "By grace are ye saved through faith; and that not of yourselves: it is the gift of God: not of works, lest any man should boast; for we are his workmanship, created in Christ Jesus unto good works, which God hath before ordained that we should walk in them" (Eph. 2. 8–10). The rite of baptism, and the theology which the New Testament attaches to it, proclaims all this with supreme clarity.

(6) *Faith, in its beliefs about God in Christ, in its trust in God's promises, and in its persevering hope of God's glory, disclaims all self-confidence, relies on God only, and praises God alone.* Trust and inner certitude, correlative to the witness of the Spirit in the heart of the believer, belong to its nature. Faith, in other words, is more than credence: it is commitment to and (to use the old word) "affiance" in God, Christ, and the promises, on the basis of credence. Faith is a complex, whole-souled response of trust in and reliance on the

gracious Christ, and the grace of that Christ in whose reality one believes. Faith is always conscious of one's own hopelessness and incapacity to save oneself; in Charles Wesley's phrase, faith is "confident in self-despair", and ever looks outside and away from a man's own self to rely on the blood and righteousness of his Saviour.

(7) *Grace is personal meeting between God and man.* This is clear from what has already been said. God lays himself open to man in the Bible, read and preached, in the sacraments duly administered, and in the worshipping fellowship of the Church; man in response lays himself open to God in prayer and fellowship with the Church. The concept of "means of grace" must be construed in personal, not mechanical, terms.

(8) *The purpose and effect of God's work of grace is to establish a redeemed community, to which he stands in covenant relation, and which he fills constantly with his Spirit.* Our view of the Church will be set forth in a later chapter, and need not therefore be dwelt on now; suffice it to say that our common vision of the Church as the Spirit-filled covenantal community seems to us both a vital emphasis for the present and a most significant growing-point for the future.

We believe that these theses should commend themselves to all biblical Christians as a sufficient confession of the truth concerning grace and justification to be a basis for a united Church.

3

Church and Sacraments

THE RESURRECTION

The present Archbishop of Canterbury has written[1] of the shock he received when as a student he started to attend the lectures of the late Sir Edwyn Hoskyns. "The lecturer began with the declaration that, as our subject was the Theology and Ethics of the New Testament, we must begin with the passages about the resurrection." This seemed to contradict all the obvious preconceptions. Surely the resurrection was the climax, the crown to the other events? No, says Dr Ramsey, "The Resurrection is a true starting-place for the study of the making and meaning of the New Testament."

If this is true for the study of the making and meaning of the New Testament it is no less true for a study of the Church and sacraments. The New Testament Church stems from the resurrection. The effect is inconceivable without the cause. Thus C. F. D. Moule writes: "If the coming into existence of the Nazarenes, a phenomenon undeniably attested in the New Testament, rips a great hole in the history, a hole of the size and shape of the resurrection, what does the secular historian propose to stop it up with?"[2] Yet Professor Moule is asserting more than cause and effect. He writes of "the extraordinary conception of the Lord Jesus Christ as a corporate, a more-than-individual personality"[3] and urges this fact upon the historian's attention. Christians from the start saw themselves as not merely following a risen Christ, but as "in" him. If God raised his Son from the dead, then he also raised his people from death to life "in" Christ. Here is God's own starting-point for our inquiry.

CHURCH, SPIRIT, AND WORD

To start with the resurrection is not to deny that the Church's origins in time lie further back. The Bible holds out to us the

---

[1] In *The Resurrection of Christ*; quotations are from Fontana edition (1961), p. 1.
[2] *The Phenomenon of the New Testament*, p. 3.   [3] Ibid., p. 23.

picture of Abraham called by God to be the father of the covenant community—a community marked out by the covenant sign of circumcision, a community given identity by the redemptive act of the Exodus and recalling this in its sacrament of the Passover, a community to live down the ages under obedience to the word of God. The New Covenant community is one in continuity with the old; it is the old olive tree with some branches broken off and other new ones incorporated. And yet there is a radical discontinuity. The new is a re-creation of the old, a re-creation effected by the resurrection—the new is "begotten again to a living hope by the resurrection of Jesus from the dead". And the new is indwelt by the Spirit of God as Pentecost follows hard on Easter and Ascension. The gift of the Spirit into the hearts is a distinctive feature of the prophecies about the new covenant (as, e.g., in Jer. 31). It is by the one Spirit that we are made one in the one Body of Christ—it is by the one Spirit that God dwells in the one temple.

We have been led to reflect on the meaning of the "temple" imagery of the Church in the New Testament. It is acknowledged that Jesus spoke of the destruction of the physical temple in Jerusalem, yet also offered to raise "this temple" again in three days— that is, the temple of his body. The physical temple then was both redundant from the time of our Lord (as that which it signified was embodied in Jesus), and was actually doomed in the economy of God to be discarded, presumably because redundant. The same two motifs apparently characterized Stephen's public ministry, heightened by his further assertion that temple-building was a mistaken preoccupation of Solomon's in the first place.

All temple typology in the sphere of sacrifice, priesthood, and access to God would seem to have been fulfilled in Jesus, according to the Letter to the Hebrews. Here the vital theme is the location of the Holy of Holies in heaven and not on earth at all. Nevertheless the discussion of these themes, though complete in itself, does not exhaust the significance of the temple typology. There remains a totally different strand of thought which by definition would be self-defeating if it were seen as fulfilled in heaven and not on earth. The temple had been the outward place of God's dwelling. In the middle of Jerusalem the guarantee of God's presence with his people could be found. Just as the pillar of cloud and fire had moved with the people of God through the wilderness, so now the tabernacle had found its permanent home and the people had to adhere to that particular place if they were to be recognizably the people of God at all.

It is exactly this set of ideas which is fulfilled and transcended in the New Testament antitypical use of the concept of the temple. If Jesus was to raise on the third day his physical body, yet was also thereafter to incorporate his followers into that body (with only a subtle widening of meaning), so on the third day he was to raise the new temple from the ground and (by precisely the same widening of meaning) build his followers into it. We are used to the imagery of the one body of the new man. This is evocative and challenging concerning our organic relationship to our head and to each other. We perhaps need a fuller grasp of this temple imagery. It would seem to be equally evocative and challenging concerning the indwelling of the glory of God in the fellowship of his people. Here is the "place" on earth where the presence of God dwells. It is a single "place"—for the temple imagery of Eph. 2 depends upon this numerical oneness. It is the place to which the heathen are to flow to find God. It is the place where true worship is to be offered. It is the place above all places to be kept pure and undefiled. The truth is not just that through Jesus God has revealed a higher dignity in man than that which he had before (though this is true). It is rather that whatever the temple meant before, a greater than the old temple has now come, superseding it and relating us to it not just as visitors accorded certain dignity by God, but as living stones built into its fabric eternally. Here by the Spirit of God the Shekinah-Glory dwells on earth.

This type of imagery—body, temple, etc.—which emphasizes the unity of the Church "in" Christ carries strong implications for our understanding of membership. If to belong to Christ in discipleship is to be "in" Christ in membership, then the members, by the sheer fact of discipleship, belong organically to each other. It is unthinkable that a man should first be converted and later "join" a, or even the, Church. As the New Testament sets out the evidence, and as the Church of the Fathers practised for centuries, a man is confronted by a community proclaiming Christ and serving him, and if he comes to believe in that Christ he comes *ipso facto* into that one community. Discipleship and membership are inseparable.

In the light of this we must reject a voluntarist understanding of the nature of the Church on earth. The Church in one place cannot in principle be formed solely by the gravitation to each other of the like-minded, nor by the association of those who happen to find the same form of worship suits them. *All* who belong to Christ belong organically to each other, and it is the task of the Church in each place to strive for a true expression of this inner reality. The goal is that the one whole body should be "joined and knit together by every joint with which it is supplied"[1]—a goal which would be not only unattainable but also undesirable on voluntarist presuppositions.[2] The organic nature of the Church in turn carries vast implications for the proper programme for church life, and for the proper procedures for implementing it. It will be possible to look later into the implications for both pluriformity and decision-taking.

None of the discussion above precludes the obvious fact that the word of God comes to an individual. It is indeed nowadays possible for it to come by radio or television to an individual totally devoid of contact with a Christian community. Nor does it preclude the obvious fact that the individual has on his own to make a decision for and by himself. Nor does it preclude the obvious fact that the word of God is creative of the Church as it touches individuals and brings them to trust in Jesus Christ. It merely asserts that the individual is *already* a member incorporated in the old man, Adam, and is by transplantation at the hands of God (working through his word and Spirit) now to be incorporated in the new man, Christ. The individual is transferred—but from one community to another. His transference in a moment of time leaves him never an atomized individual.

CHURCH AND SACRAMENTS

It has frequently been observed that what a man takes for granted may be of more significance than what he fervently affirms. Certainly it is right to examine St Paul's writings in this way. Not every belief or practice of the Church in his time was being called in question in such a way as to make it central to an argument by the Apostle. Much is taken for granted and simply provides the framework within which he writes his polemical or corrective material. His presuppositions are the point at issue when

---

[1] Eph. 4. 16.
[2] It would of course be easy to show that the opposite error—the Vatican I "juridical" understanding—has the same ultimate effect.

A. M. Hunter writes: "St Paul did not invent or introduce the rites of Baptism or the Lord's Supper. He found them already existing. There is no evidence that he radically transformed these pre-Pauline rites."[1] To this we may add another point. There was simply no need for St Paul to write treatises on these rites to correct prevalent errors—hence he did not. And thus in turn his mention of them is almost entirely allusive. He takes them entirely for granted. They must therefore have been matters of agreement in the Church from the start, stemming from the resurrection, ascension, and Pentecost. And this too our limited historical evidence attests.

Three great doctrinal points unite these two sacraments of the new covenant, and merit further discussion.

First, both sacraments declare Jesus' death and resurrection and mediate to us both their benefits and their challenge. We shall go on to urge that the benefits and the challenge are simply one. We now cite as evidence Rom. 6. 1–7 in the case of baptism, and the tension in John 6. 51–8 between the feeding on Christ himself and the feeding on his body and blood in the case of the Eucharist. If this were to be relevant after the resurrection (let alone in the time it was written, many decades later) it would speak simultaneously of Jesus' death and resurrection. From death to life—for Jesus and for us in him—this is the great common theme of both sacraments.

Secondly, both sacraments relate to the organic corporate character of the Church. The Church is formed as a unity by baptism. On a universal scale this is expressed in the concept of being baptized by one Spirit into one body (1 Cor. 12. 13). In the microcosm of the local church it is expressed in the appeal of St Paul to the fact of baptism into the name of Christ as a preservative against schism (1 Cor. 1). In baptism not only is the individual submitting to Christ, but the Church is extending her frontiers, incorporating another captive of the gospel into the body of Christ. Without baptism there may or may not be individuals with a personal devotion to the Christ of the Scriptures, but there is no scriptural church, no Body of Christ on earth.

The same is in its way true of the Eucharist. The references in Acts 2, 1 Cor. 10, and 1 Cor. 11 all attest in passing the corporate character of the meal. If the Church's frontiers are set by baptism they are reaffirmed by communion. The excommunicate and the

---

[1] *Paul and his Predecessors* (S.C.M. 1961), p. 110.

non-communicant alike are outside the fellowship. The day-to-day unity of the Church is given and revealed in the week-to-week communion of the people of God.

Thirdly, both sacraments bear the same relationship as each other to faith and to God's grace. The Reformers' instinct to treat them under one head was clearly right. The language of Scripture about them is the language of sheer unqualified efficacy. If the outward celebration is performed, then on the first showing the inward grace is mediated. Those who have been baptized into Christ "have put on Christ" (Gal. 3. 27). Those who receive communion receive the body and blood of Christ (as the words of institution testify). The simple expectation is that those who partake of the sacraments are partakers in them and by them of God's grace. If there is an occasional warning, such as in 1 Cor. 10, yet the overall picture is one of serene objectivity and confidence on the writers' part in the efficacy of the sacraments.

The traditional Protestant reply to such a conclusion would have been to say that faith was taken for granted, and "in such only as worthily receive the same they have a wholesome effect or operation".[1] The Protestant could go on to urge that the same results were attributable to God's word and Spirit without mention of the sacraments (as, e.g., in 1 Pet. 1. 23 "Born anew of the... word"), and that, as the word was the primary means of God's work of salvation, the reputed efficacy of the sacraments in the New Testament could only be understood as dependent upon a prior acceptance of the word of God by faith.

No final resolution of this problem lies ready to hand. The sacraments are other than acted exhortations (which is how extreme Protestants have sometimes explained them). They are equally other than alchemical panaceas for all woes (as Catholicism has sometimes tended to assume). We dare not argue as to which comes first, the sacrament or the faith. Without faith it is true that a sacrament is not in itself salvific. Without the sacraments it is true that the Church has no warrant for treating men and women as in Christ. The two simply belong together. If the sacraments are to be placed alongside the word then they are comparable to the word administered *and received*, not simply to the word as preached. Even this leaves us short of the truth. They are comparable to the word apprehending people for God for specified reasons. And they

[1] Article 25.

are not replaceable by the word, for they are themselves part of the message of the word (which would by definition be stunted without them), they are formative of the society we call the Church (which the word cannot be without them), and they constitute fulcra upon which the word can be placed to lever the people of God forward in their earthly pilgrimage. And here again the two sacraments are patient of a single treatment.

THE SACRAMENTS AND CREATION

It is germane to the discussion to ask, Why material elements? No doubt God in his wisdom can simply choose to use his creation without deigning to give us reasons, yet we discern certain principles at work in his choice which may give the clue to answer the question. One such main principle is his consistent will to work through the particular to bring about the universal. This is observable as applied to people, to places, and to things.

The sacraments of the new covenant embody this principle, for they take over existing rites and give them new meaning and effect. They involve the use of the created world in the shape of water, bread, and wine. However great may be the spiritual significance we ought to ascribe to them, yet their sheer physical nature and use must not be obscured or overlooked. It overthrows the nature of a sacrament as much to spiritualize it by nullifying any real significance in the physical aspect, as to remove its sacramental nature by identifying that which is signified with its sacramental manifestation. Baptism is still a literal physical washing. The Eucharist is still a real eating and drinking, and the sacramental bread and wine still nourish our bodies.

But the significance lies deeper also. The re-creation of man effected in and by Christ is a re-creation of the whole man—body, mind, and spirit. On beyond this there lies the re-creation of the whole physical world mysteriously bound in with our redemption. The creation was made subject to vanity in and through the fall of man. It is to be freed from its bondage to corruption in the wake of the eschatological revealing of the sons of God. Thus God uses the physical as a means of grace to us, partly in order that he may use us as a means of grace to the physical creation. Re-creation both here and to come exemplifies God's use of the particular for the sake of the universal.

BAPTISM

Baptism is once-for-all initiation into Christ. It is certainly capable of much exposition, but it is equally certainly not less than this. In the New Testament the main fact that is stressed is not simply that we are united with Christ, important though that is, but that we are united with him through death to life. We have adumbrated this point above, but it cannot be too strongly emphasized. Baptism has twin foci of "death to life"—first Jesus' death and resurrection, from which both faith and sacrament take their origin, and then ours, which is a death to sin and a new life of righteousness. The foci belong with each other, but are to be kept severely distinct. We have no sacrifice to make like his—he has no sin or need of new righteousness like us.

In the Bible, faith stands in opposition to sin. Sin originates in a refusal to depend on God (an aggressive no-faith), but results not only in alienation of man from God, but also of man from man, of man from creation, and of man within himself. Adam and Eve are banished from the garden, committed to often fruitless toil, and are swiftly followed by the murder of Abel and the confusion of Babel. The condition of fallen man within himself is vividly portrayed in St Paul's words "The good that I would, that I do not; and the evil that I would not, that I do" (Rom. 7. 19).

Just as sin is corporate, so is its counterpart, faith. The individual is born in sin, in the corrupt and condemned body of Adam. If he is to be united with Christ, then it will be in his life-giving justified body. Baptism and faith only unite us with Christ in his death and resurrection by incorporating us into the one body. The individual enters thus upon a *corporate* life—the life of the Church. Here is the sphere within which is being worked out the restoration of the unity between man and God, the unity between man and man, as also seminally between man and creation and (often quite notably) within man himself. The individual has no warrant for looking for this restoration outside the unity of the one Body of Christ which he enters at baptism. And equally a theology of baptism which ignores the corporate implications of faith is as much a distortion of the New Testament teaching as any concept of faith which isolates or atomizes the individual.

We may note in passing that the Church of England's Catechism (along with other Reformation-period formularies) culpably

57

individualizes the death-to-life aspect of baptism.[1] In the opening section there is more emphasis on becoming a "member of Christ", but in the section on the sacraments alone does this death-to-life aspect arise, and then only in an individualistic and moral way. A reintegration of the baptismal teaching of the Catechism would require that "member of Christ" should be spelled out in a more corporate way, and that the death-to-life theme should be closely related to this corporate understanding. Thus the opening would be preserved from distortion into the attitude "We have Abraham for our father", and the later treatment would be rooted in a properly corporate context. The Revised Catechism is better.

In short, submission to baptism is integral to submission to the gospel.[2] The gospel makes us one in the Second Adam by baptism. The unbaptized Christian is not only unprecedented in Scripture —he is also an individual flying in the face of the corporate meaning of the gospel.

HOLY COMMUNION

It is clear from the New Testament that the characteristic act of those who had been baptized into Christ was to join in the breaking of the bread. Indeed, without straining the evidence it can be said that the Christian life can be described scripturally as living out the meaning of our baptism by taking part in the Lord's Supper. Such a description assumes that the corporate meaning of baptism is faithfully reproduced in the Lord's Supper, an assumption fully warranted by the New Testament.

The corporateness of this distinctive act lies not in the mere shepherding into one service at one time of as large a congregation as possible (for this might be primarily an expression of purely human fellowship). There *is* a strong case for togetherness in the sacrament, and there can be no sacrament at all without at least a microcosm of the local church present. But that is not the point. Just as we share one common baptism, uniting us in one body of Christ and building us into the one temple, so we share one common

---

[1] But contrast Article 26 of 1553, "Our Lorde Jesus Christe hathe knitte toguether a companie of newe people with Sacramentes..."

[2] Children of Christian homes are only to be baptized as those who are involved in their families' submission to the gospel. The specific doctrinal case for infant baptism is too long and large a matter to set out here, and it is not well served by a less than full statement. We are agreed about the propriety of infant baptism, though we have not had opportunity to discuss it among ourselves with the fullness it merits.

loaf, thus sustaining our unity in the body and in the temple. The Eucharist is the proclamation of Christ's death as the means of our discipleship and incorporation, but this means that it is the sacrament in which we are newly re-apprehended by Christ and thus enabled by his grace to live out the death-to-life of our baptism. The Eucharist is placed in the tension typical of Christians themselves—a sign simultaneously of the past work of Christ on Calvary, from which the community takes its origin, and of the present reign and lordship of the risen Christ who in person presides over the community and purifies it in the way of discipleship. The sacrament has also that eschatological expectation which is supposed to characterize the people of God. All these three aspects of it are set out objectively in the celebration of the Eucharist. It is their sheer objectivity which arouses devotion—their proclamation is in no sense dependent upon the state of mind or heart in which the worshippers assemble for the service.

We have to ask in what sense the Eucharist can be called a sacrifice. A technical discussion of the significance of the elements as signs and as related to the sacrifice of Christ is offered elsewhere.[1] But it is germane to the present discussion to consider the relevance of self-offering by the worshippers. Catholic and Evangelical alike, we are all concerned to proclaim the uniqueness of Calvary and the total dependence of man upon God's redeeming acts. No offering we can make must appear to rival or dim these great facts. Yet we are a Christian priesthood in our corporate unity, and there is surely a sacrifice of some sort we are to offer as priests?

Here the idea that we have nothing to offer, merely something to receive, traditionally stands over against the concept that somehow we offer a sacrifice which is in itself pleasing to God. We must reject this harsh polarization, but the question presses, what *can* we offer at the Eucharist? Not mere bread and wine—even the term "offertory" sounds an odd note; not merely "the fruit of our lips"; not merely undefined "spiritual sacrifices"; not merely ourselves, considered apart from Christ; not even ourselves in Christ, if that is seen in separation from our feeding on Christ; but ourselves as reappropriated by Christ. If the sacrament is to communicate to us afresh the benefits of Christ's passion, then we must reaffirm quickly that it also communicates to us the demands of it. It may be

[1] See Appendix 4.

59

good liturgically to express our self-offering as responsive to God's grace (by putting the prayer of self-oblation after communion), but there is no real time sequence to be represented. If God's grace in the sacrament is as much God re-apprehending us for his service as it is God conveying comfort and relief, then the sacrifice of ourselves, though logically dependent upon the re-mediated salvation, is contemporaneous with the reception and is only put after communion as a linguistic device expressing that logical dependence. It is indeed arguable that the very mission of the Church has been less hindered in the Church of England by the recurrence of late medieval theories of re-offering Christ than by the prevalent comfort-and-relief concept of reception. If we come to communion already in Christ, yet our reintegration with each other in communion is also a reintegration in Christ's mission.

If communion is this reintegration with each other in Christ, then it is clear that the nature of the Church on earth is closely bound up with its practice of communion. The Church to be one on earth ought to be in communion with itself. Yet a *de facto* local division into two produces a situation where the purpose of communion is frustrated before any joint communion is joined. This is more or less the situation adumbrated in 1 Cor. 11—a situation where, without the deep mutual commitment to each other in Christ that an organic understanding of the church implies, communion was becoming an empty husk of unity. Though St Paul apparently solves the issue by a temporary interdict from any sacrament, yet when a deep rift has occurred with ramifications all over Christendom it would not necessarily be wise to tell all to abstain from the sacrament until a reintegration can be attained. But it does mean that we cannot merely say that indiscriminate intercommunion will answer all our ecumenical problems.[1]

It is arguable as a consequence of this doctrine of the Eucharist that it is illogical to admit children to baptism in infancy but deny them communion until puberty. The children (it would be said) are reckoned to be in the community for the purposes of baptism but are not taken seriously as the baptized thereafter. If it be argued that adult or near-adult faith and discernment is needed for communion, it can be replied that parity of reasoning would demolish infant baptism. If children are in the community with and through their parents, then they should be in the community meal, re-

---

[1] For further discussion of this see Appendix 3.

incorporated into Christ, with their parents also. The Church of England shows some signs of awaking to serious reflection on this thesis at the time of writing. Perhaps it is a point for radical reform on the occasion of reunion.

SACRAMENTS AND ORDER

We must now set out three important points about the context within which the sacraments are to be celebrated: the conditions under which they are celebrated, the responsibility for having them celebrated, and the minister of the celebrations.

As to the first of these, we must revert to the doctrine of justification. When the Church celebrates the sacraments it is concerned to obey the commands of the Lord. Its task is to perform the acts through which our Lord has promised to act towards his new covenant people. To put it negatively, there is no question of the Church's performing either an act which is meritorious in itself or an act as a result of which, through the merit of the participants, it hopes to win some benefit from God. In the sacraments the Church, in obedience, faith, and humility, acts in reliance upon our Lord's promise and power, not presumptuously but confident that he will not fail us. The need for our response must be constantly set before us, but we are not to make our sincerity or degree of understanding the basic condition for his acting. If we dodge the questions What does our Lord tell us to do? and How has the Church to put this into practice?, we run the risk of doing what our faith (or our need, or worse, our sentiment) suggests and of relying upon our sincerity to ensure that God does his part. Unless we are concerned to obey our Lord under the new covenant, we shall be standing the sacraments upon their heads and turning them into cultic rites devised by the Church to help man find God (and expendable if they don't!).

As to the second point, the responsibility for the celebrations, if it be granted that the sacraments are church acts with strong ecclesial significance, then the responsibility lies with the Church. General rules may well be made at diocesan, provincial, or higher level, but their application is and must be the responsibility of the local community. The times and frequency of services, the forms and texts, and furnishings and music—all these should be congregationally determined. To deliver the responsibility for the sacraments into the hands of the minister alone is to run dangerously near to treating the sacraments as medicines dispensed by an expert doctor at his sole discretion. If their churchly character is to emerge, then the minister and laity must act together in determining the best context for the celebrations.

This raises the third point. If the responsibility for providing the sacraments is a corporate one, who is to minister them? Here the case for an (or the) ordained ministry of the sacraments is strong. If there is a single actual celebrant functioning on behalf of the whole church which is involved in the celebration, then he should, it would appear, be a public officer of the Church. This is the best expression the Church can give to the two earlier points about context made above. If the celebration is to be obedience not whim, this obedience is best represented by the celebrant being one appointed by the Church to act in this capacity: a celebrant who took the task upon himself would rather tend to reflect the whim, albeit the sincere whim, of the individual. The corporate ecclesial character of the celebration will be best represented by the same provision: celebration by a private individual would rather tend towards schism or at least sacramental cliquishness. We can at this stage of our argument put these points no higher than "would rather tend", as the New Testament gives no direct guidance on the question. (Some theological considerations pointing in a particular direction will be mentioned in the next chapter.)

THE CHURCH AND ITS UNITY

From this sacramental background arise certain consequences for the Church in pursuit of visible unity.[1]

First, the unity of the Church is all of a piece with its holiness. We are in danger of sundering these two attributes of the Church too severely, and thus being able to pursue one independently of the other. (This is a danger only exceeded by *equating* the one with the other—as though the Church's sole goal on earth were to be visibly one.) Our holiness is another way of looking at our willingness to

[1] Cf. the Keele declaration of April 1967: "[Unity] is not the only goal required of us. We must emphasise also the need to love and hold fast to the truth, to pursue holiness, and to practise evangelism. To join together divided Christians in a way that would compromise these other ideals would be to miss God's will and to retard his work. So we dare not accept uncritically any and every proposed means to unity" (*Keele '67*, para. 81).

be apprehended by the truth as it is in Jesus. It seems very arguable that a quest for unity which outruns the quest for holiness may in the end be frighteningly self-defeating. It is perhaps to this fact that St Paul draws attention when he says that "there must be heresies among you in order that those who are genuine may be recognised" (1 Cor. 11. 19, R.S.V.)—that is, we may properly, yet with divine discontent, accept a degree of disunity commensurate with our unholiness or we may obscure the degree of truth and obedience we already have. This we believe to be a timely reminder in a day when unity seems so often the sole goal in view.

Secondly, the unity and holiness of the Church are all of a piece with its mission. The Church is to be a community proclaiming Jesus Christ by lip and by life. The Church which is constituted by the sacraments is God's mission on earth. There is no static holiness in view, any more than a static unity. The whole goal of unity-in-holiness must be infused with the sense of a Church purified and more clearly Spirit-filled in order to serve God on earth. Just as we have no patience with the view that we have no message or mission to the world until the outward disunity is healed, so we have equally no patience with the view that unity itself will be a sufficient message to the world.[1] If God calls his people to be one, they must not stay on the enjoyment of a unity which might run dangerously near to mere cosiness, but must see their unity as God's enabling of them to pursue his mission in the world. If Jesus prayed that his people should be one, he did so in order that the message might reach the world "that the world may know that you have sent me" (John 17. 23). Here is a continuing, demanding theological task of proclamation. Unity by itself would be a false crest which should give us little sense of attainment, and might prove, like a false crest, a discouragement as much as an encouragement. We have to continue the climb and have to go towards unity—but we must recognize the danger of it being a false crest now, lest the disappointment at the time be great.

Thirdly, the unity of the Church in visible terms is to be sought particularly in the local community. It may be of little consequence whether or not Christians in Zanzibar are in full fellowship with those in the Arctic, but it is certainly of profound importance whether the Christians in one village or small town are divided

---

[1] The world may equally view bare uniting as an admission of sheer weakness —unity of itself carries no clear message at all.

from each other. The eucharistic assembly which is supposed to characterize and sustain the Church's unity will seem a contradiction in terms if there is another such assembly across the road. One of our great troubles in England today is that the local Christian community has little chance to feel itself the body of Christ in an area; it is too split for the Christians in one street even to recognize each other, let alone for there to be a true care of the sick, the backsliding, the social needs. The whole thrust of 1 Corinthians is opposed to local division. The whole practice of the early Church stands as a similar witness. The comity agreements of the nineteenth-century missionary movements in Asia and Africa tell the same story.[1] No one starting the Church again from scratch could possibly contemplate setting up denominations opposed to each other in the same locality. Thus if arguments are advanced for keeping the present divided position they are, *prima facie*, rationalizations.[2] We declare ourselves, even after the cautions given above, as passionately concerned for the union of local Christian communities.

Fourthly, we declare our concern that unity should exhibit and retain diversity. If the body of Christ has many differing members, our church life should do full justice to that. No doubt there are differences among members in which one is right and one sinful. The nature of church life must promote the healthy living together of such members (with a view to a better mind prevailing). But there are also differences simply deriving from the fact that God by nature and by grace has given different gifts to his different children, and he desires his Church to conserve and exploit the rich variety of abilities contained within it. A local church may have to join together in worship, and it is difficult to imagine everyone worshipping in different ways simultaneously. But in almost every other task the formation of a community mind and outlook need not involve uniformity at all. The crucial point is that the doctrine of the many members in one body should be held before people's eyes as an incentive to true love and a refraining from coercion.

[1] This was true even where the societies had strong theological disagreements with each other. They could view others as sufficiently Christian to be entitled to work in an area without opposing communities having to be set up against them. Thus one part of India could be Anglican, another Baptist.

[2] The most obvious is that we all have different psychologies, and therefore need a choice between different types of worship from which to choose. This is hopelessly voluntarist, foreign to the New Testament, and unfair on the Indians who were never given the local choice!

What is true between the members locally is also true as between the several congregations which may be knit together in a diocese or other unit. Their organic relationship does not imply any uniformity. At this point there may even be opportunity for great differences (such as those culturally determined) between forms of worship used. As each local community has the task of local mission as a great priority in its life, so each must have great liberty in determining for itself the forms of church life best suited to its local calling. We later[1] state our conviction that on the present English scene it is right to examine whether the local church has not a decisively self-determining role to play in the question of whether, when, and on what terms, it should be involved in a union scheme. This we believe to be a proper attribution to the local church of the responsibility for its own life which the New Testament accords it.

Lastly, this very decision brings us to consider the implications for the Church of the connection between unity and authority. The local church is called upon by Paul to expel a member, to correct its eucharistic practice, to take up monetary collections, and so on. The original authority for such commands may be apostolic, but that is not the point. It is the task of the church (universal and local) in each generation to receive the apostolic word and live under it by implementing it in its own ongoing life. No doubt the initiative in such implementation lies with church officers, ministers, or leaders. But the responsibility belongs in the last analysis to all the members, just because they are one. And it is a proper reflection of our stated conviction that the Church, however weak or sinful, is the Spirit-filled body of Christ, if we look for a general consensus of policy in regard to the policies by which the word is implemented. Reaching a consensus may be a slow and costly process, yet to pre-empt the process is to call in question our doctrine of the Church. Thus if the Church is to move in major doctrinal questions (such as are involved in union schemes), an organic consensus must be looked for in every unit to be involved. If this suggests that no such consensus up and down the country can be realistically envisaged in the next century (whilst organic unity presses as an urgent priority), then the conclusion may well be drawn that unions should be attempted at a lowlier level than that of the whole country at once. Such a way of reunion would involve

---

[1] See pp. 132–3.

both the principle of diversity between congregations, *and* the general consensus of those involved. It would be a merciful deliverance from the threats of not an infallible pope but at least an infallible 75 %.

Baptism was described in the discussion above as "once-for-all initiation into Christ". This is demanded by the theology of the New Testament with its insistence on a single transition from darkness to light, from Adam to Christ. It is therefore almost impossible to break up the inner meaning of initiation in order to allocate one part of it to water and another to the laying on of hands or anointing.

We have not, in any case, examined the question of what is included in the word "baptism" in the New Testament. Yet we cannot see that the New Testament or post-apostolic Church presents an invariable pattern of water-and-laying-on-of-hands for initiation, though the water is invariable. The lacunae about the second ceremony are legion. The Acts of the Apostles has nine occasions of baptism in water, only two of laying on of hands. St Paul has frequent reference to water-baptism, arguably none at all (or only one in the Pastorals) to laying on of hands. The Letter to the Hebrews has one tantalizing mention of the laying on of hands (though no discussion of the significance of it), and the rest of the New Testament none at all. Much further study is needed as to what the word "baptism" should be held to include.

Further, assuming that there are various elements and that they can be distinguished, the question must be asked, How far is it logically possible to defer part of the sacrament of *initiation*?

The resolution of these points cannot be secured overnight and we are not convinced that a solution is essential to a scheme of union. Nevertheless, there are certain points which we believe must be secured, not least because of the problems presented by infant baptism.

First, we hold fast to the principle of baptizing the infants of Christian families in water. We should expect that, in a Church ruled by a rigorous theological logic, only communicants would qualify their infants for baptism. Children would then be eligible for admission to communion with their parents.

Secondly, we see need for those baptized as infants to make some adult profession of their baptismal faith when they come to years of discretion. What those years are should be determined partly by sociological factors (school-leaving age, voting age, etc.). The age adopted for this would in principle be also the minimum age for baptism of those from non-Christian homes—the youngest age at which the person could be deemed to be acting as an independent, fully responsible adult. This would of course be long after the admission of children of Christian homes to communion, and once it was detached from admission to communion it would not be hard to postpone it beyond the present age of puberty (and indiscretion?). The ratification of baptismal faith in this way might or might not be accompanied by the laying on of hands, but it would be done in the presence of the bishop.

What is essential is that it should be presented and understood as an expression of life in Christ to be effected by the enabling of the Holy Spirit. It is only too easy for it to be understood as a Pelagian act of self-effort. The New Testament pattern must be maintained, by which the human act is seen as a response to the calling of God and dependent for its fulfilment upon the working of the Holy Spirit.

Thirdly, we cannot regard those who are to be baptized as adults as needing any ceremony other than water-baptism before entry into the communicant life, provided that the bishop is presiding at their initiation and the Eucharist which should follow. This practice of the bishop presiding should be regarded as the normal one. If, for some exceptional reason, the bishop could not be present, the newly initiated should be received into fellowship by the bishop as soon as possible. This could take the form of the laying on of hands. We cannot view those who have received water-baptism in other denominations without further ceremony as not having received Christian initiation, but their entry into a united Church would involve their acceptance of the need for communion with the bishop as both symbol and sustainer of the unity of the Church.

Fourthly, we believe that the Anglican practice of confirmation, whatever its anomalies and weaknesses as currently manifested, has one important pastoral (and theologically significant) side to it which we would urge should be conserved in any change of practice. Confirmation at the moment is administered to all Anglicans by a bishop, and each recipient is thus brought (at the point of admission to communion) into direct and visible communion with the bishop. The bishop's function as both symbol and sustainer of the Church's unity is worked out most evocatively and helpfully in this way, and it is a question of how it could be maintained. A smaller diocese (such as is advocated in chs. 8 and 9) might lead to the following practice:

(a) The infant would usually be baptized by the local presbyter (though exceptionally the bishop might officiate). His communion with the church local and universal would be mediated through his parents or guardians, and it would be *their* place in the church which would safeguard his. On reaching years of discretion he would be recognized and accepted as an adult by the bishop (at a service perhaps not unlike the present Confirmation), and would thus hold his place in the Church both by being an adult believer and by his relationship with the bishop.

(b) The adult, as shown just above, would be baptized and communicated by the bishop himself in person at a single service of initiation. He would come into direct relationship with the bishop.

(c) If households were baptized, or other infants with the adults, then the bishop would also baptize infants and perhaps children on such occasions.

(d) Those baptized, whether as infants or adults, in other denominations would be received into fellowship by the bishop at a communion service at which he would preside.

Thus all adults would be in immediate relation with the bishop, and this particular valuable feature of present Anglican practice would be preserved.

4

Episcopacy and Ministry

THE CHURCH'S CONTEXT IN HISTORY

In this chapter we are primarily concerned with the Church militant here on earth. When we were baptized into Christ we became members of the One Holy Catholic Apostolic Church, stretching beyond the grave into the world to come. We were made one with Christ and the whole company of the redeemed. We became citizens of heaven. Yet until we die we are members of that part of it which is still on earth and which we do well to remember is the smaller part. We are members of a visible, concrete society. It is visible in that it is composed of living men and women, of flesh and blood. It is a society with a history stretching back to the events in history which reformed the people of God, Israel, and so brought into being the New Israel, the Church. It is a society with a declared belief in the meaning of those events both for itself and for the whole of mankind.

As a visible society, it looks in two directions. It looks back to those events in history and their meaning as set out in Scripture and in the tradition of the Church guided by the Spirit. It also looks in obedience to the risen, living Christ, active in his Church to nourish, correct, and sustain those who are united to him, that it may be the instrument for proclaiming the gospel. At the same time the Church militant is under pressure from the world to be conformed to its thought and judgement. One effect of this pressure has been that the Church has tried to divorce the two directions in which it must look simultaneously. So we find on the one hand attempts simply to look back to the past, with a narrow concentration on historical events to the exclusion of the living Christ. On the other hand we find attempts to reduce the life of the Church to a "mystery religion based upon spiritual experience uncontrolled by the death of Jesus and by his teaching and action", to quote Sir Edwyn Hoskyns.[1] When a spirit of religion is abroad, as, for example, in the first or seventeenth centuries, such attempts result

---

[1] *The Apostolicity of the Church*, A Report of the Anglo-Catholic Conference, 1930 (C.L.A.), p. 89.

in a form of natural religion such as Gnosticism or Deism, which has little to do with the gospel of the New Testament. When, as in our present age, in this century, any idea of religion is alien to the majority of people, it results in the substitution of a temporal gospel for the New Testament proclamation of eternal life in Christ which begins in this world and is fulfilled in the world to come. It results in the all too evident spectacle of the Church attempting the impossible task of justifying its existence and purpose on the world's terms. The phenomena change, but the cause is the same—the predicament of an uncontrolled "spiritual" religion is already to be seen in the Church of the New Testament. The dangers of a mystery religion based on spiritual experience lie behind the teaching in the Epistles of St John. St Paul, in his letter to the Church at Corinth, is concerned to recall it to the significance of the resurrection and the Last Supper and to the way in which the behaviour of Christians must be controlled by these events.

THE FUNCTION OF THE MINISTRY

The teaching of St Paul and St John in the face of these problems is that the function of the ministry is to exercise a pastoral care in the name and power of Christ by which the obedience of the Church to the living Christ is controlled and disciplined by the events which brought it into being. In other words, it is in the ministry of the Church that the two directions in which the Church must look are focused. It is the duty of those called to oversight to minister in Christ's name for the edification of the Church. It is equally their duty to witness to the apostolic faith and to secure that the life of the Church is firmly rooted in the events of our redemption.

This primary function of the ministry is seen not only in the New Testament but in the earliest accounts we have of the functions of bishops. In the letters of St Ignatius of Antioch, who was martyred about A.D. 110, we find him exhorting the Christians to be faithful to the one Eucharist presided over by the bishop and exhorting them not to be perverted by strange doctrines which deny that Jesus truly lived and suffered and died. The two exhortations are inextricably interwoven in all his letters and link faithfulness to the gospel with communion with the bishop in the one Eucharist.[1]

---

[1] As, for example, in *Smyrnaeans* 7–9. Note that in *Smyrnaeans* 6 the word *bebaios* is usually translated "valid", but this would seem to be an anachron-

THE STRUCTURE OF THE MINISTRY

The fact that the ministry has this particular responsibility in the Church does not, of course, mean that the whole burden of maintaining the faith fell upon it. The sacraments, the Scriptures, and, at a later date, the creeds, all played their part in the presentation of the faith and in the implementation of the unity of the Church. None of them was wholly successful. Some Christians, as Ignatius made clear in his time, because of their desire to escape from the "flesh and blood" of the historical Jesus,[1] have been led to abstain from the Eucharist and to establish spiritual sects. Others have treated the Scriptures in cavalier fashion, whether by relegating them to playing a minor role or by treating them in isolation from the Church and interpreting them in accordance with what are essentially non-scriptural criteria. In like manner the ministry has become corrupted, both in the way in which it has been exercised and in the way in which it has been regarded. Proud prelates and autocratic ministers are familiar figures. What are less familiar, though equally dangerous, are views of the ministry which are contrary to the New Testament pattern. On the one hand, the view of the ministry which sees it purely in terms of a delegation by the Church of certain functions disregards the authority of the ministry to act in the name of Christ as Head of the Church for its edification. On the other hand, the view which isolates the ministry from the Church and which sees it as existing prior to the Church and thereby creating it is a grand distortion of the New Testament pattern. The New Testament teaches that not only are both minister and laity together under the gospel and under the judgement of God, but that ministry, Scriptures, and the sacraments are equally integral parts of the structure given to the Church to enable it to be faithful to and to realize its true nature.

It is worth commenting at this point on the views of the ministry set out in the proposed Scheme for Anglican–Methodist Unity (pp. 24–5). Whether or not the various views are adequately expressed is not in question here. The point is that, even if it is true

ism in which a later meaning of the word is read back. *Bebaios* can mean "steadfast", and it is argued that this is the meaning intended by Ignatius. The contrast is then between the one Eucharist of those who are with the bishop faithful and steadfast to the true gospel, and any other Eucharists that might be celebrated in isolation by those who caused schism by following strange doctrines.   [1] *Smyrnaeans* 6.

(para. 77) that the views of priesthood and ministry fall within the limits of the liberty of interpretation referred to in para. 67, no one of them adequately reflects the New Testament understanding of the ministry, and it is significant that the question is not even asked as to whether they do. There is no attempt to ask what element of New Testament truth either view is concerned to maintain, even if the defence of that truth has led to a lack of balance and to distortion.

THE MINISTRY IN A DIVIDED CHURCH— THREE QUESTIONS

When the nature of the ministry is being considered in the light of the divided state of the Church militant, three questions have to be considered:

1. What is said in the New Testament about the appointment of ministers in the Church?

2. What is the relationship between the New Testament ministry and the subsequent episcopate?

3. What is the relationship between the existing non-episcopal ministries and the episcopate?

QUESTION I: THE APPOINTMENT OF MINISTERS

As to the first question, concerning the appointment of ministers, the New Testament evidence is sparse and incidental, and there are many gaps in it, which scholars have filled with speculations of different sorts. It is a fact, however, that in each case recorded of authority and responsibility for oversight (*episkope*) being given, it is given by persons who already possess and are exercising it themselves. Passages like Rom. 12 and 1 Cor. 12 give evidence of a wide variety of occasional ministries in the first Christian communities, all of them gifts of Christ through the Holy Spirit for building up the Church's life. These modes of ministry overlap and shade into each other; every Christian takes his share in them, one way or another, and there is no reason to regard the passages referred to, or any others, as giving us an exhaustive list of the forms that these ministrations took. But they are all to be distinguished from the regular exercise of *episkope* by apostles, presbyter-bishops, and *ad hoc* apostolic nominees like Timothy and Titus. The basis of the informal and occasional ministries was the spontaneous prompting of the Spirit within, but the basis for exercising *episkope* was appointment—at least, in all the cases known to us. Our Lord appointed the Apostles (Mark 3. 14 ff; Luke 6. 13 ff). In Acts 6 the seven men chosen by the people for the service (*diakonia*) of poor relief (itself a form of *episkope*, oversight and care) were set apart by prayer and the laying on of hands by the Apostles. The presbyter-bishops of the four Asia Minor churches were appointed by Paul and Barnabas (Acts 14. 23). Timothy was appointed to minister at Ephesus by St Paul, and the gift of God that was in him for this ministry was given through "the laying on of hands of the presbytery" (1 Tim. 4. 14). Titus was similarly appointed by Paul to set things in order in Crete, and to "appoint elders in every city" (Titus 1. 5). We should note Paul's evident belief that the Holy Spirit acted in and through these appointments; this belief is apparent from his description of the presbyters of Ephesus as those whom *the Holy Spirit* had made *episkopoi*, to feed the flock of God (Acts 20. 28). At the same time, while admitting that the evidence does not allow us to assert that all presbyter-bishops without exception in apostolic times were appointed by apostles or persons commissioned by apostles (this, though not impossible, is unproveable, and perhaps unlikely), we must give due weight to the obvious fact that the commissioning of overseers by those who themselves exercised oversight already was assumed without argument to be right and proper, at least wherever it was possible.

The ministerial commission to exercise *episkope* is not the same thing as the privilege of being kings and priests to God through incorporation into Christ, for this privilege of royal priesthood belongs to every Christian as such. It is an appointment to *office*— that is, to fulfil specified functions with authority. This is clearest in the case of the Apostles themselves. Jesus, the archetypal Apostle ("sent one"), who as such is the substance of our profession (Heb. 3. 1), sent the Twelve, and later Paul, to fulfil in his name, that is as his plenipotentiary representatives, a ministry of witness to God and service to men which not only mirrored, but actually embodied and prolonged, his own ministry which he fulfilled in the days of his flesh. To his followers, he was, is, and always will be "the chief Shepherd", "the Shepherd and Bishop (*episkopos*) of your souls", "that great shepherd of the sheep" (1 Pet. 5. 4, 2. 25;

Heb. 13. 20); and the Apostles appear as under-shepherds, exercising his authority as they themselves submit to it. In this, the Apostles set the pattern for all bishops and presbyters in all ages. As eyewitnesses of the risen Christ and scribes of the New Testament, the Apostles were unique and their functions by definition untransferable, but as shepherds of God's flock, teaching and ruling, exercising oversight by instruction and discipline, they fulfilled a ministry which was archetypal and normative for all who would ever be commissioned to *episkope* in Christ's Church. So when St Peter exhorts elders to be faithful shepherds, he does so "as a fellow elder" (1 Pet. 5. 1, R.S.V.)—more than an elder, no doubt, but not less. And the authority whereby both he and they exercise *episkope* over the flock is the authority of the chief Shepherd, who has charged each of them, no less directly than he charged Peter, to "feed my sheep", and who will one day take account of them all (cf. v. 4). Thus we may say that all ministerial oversight embodies an authority which stems from Christ as Head of the Church, and witnesses to his Lordship over his Church, including its ministers themselves. And we may further say that, though New Testament presbyter-bishops were not Apostles, just as present-day bishops and presbyters are not Apostles, yet the authority of their office was identical with the authority exercised by the Apostles—namely, the personal authority of the Lord.

This is surely the reason why in New Testament times it seemed natural and right for ministerial commission to be conferred in the Church by those who already held it themselves. What this continuity of commission proclaims is not that Christ withholds his authority from any who are not commissioned in this way, but that Christ, the Church's faithful and consistent Lord, does actually confer on each new candidate for *episkope* the same authority as he conferred on those who went before in the same task.

So there is more than simply a difference of function between ordained ministers and other churchmen, and the assertion of Tillich that a minister is simply a layman with a special job to do, who differs from other laymen only by his professional training, cannot be accepted. And when Bernard Manning, the Congregationalist, affirms that a minister at ordination receives Christ's commission, not that of the congregation, we must press the question, "Do you mean a commission which Christ gives to all Christians, or his specific commission of apostolic oversight?"

QUESTION 2: THE APOSTOLATE AND EPISCOPATE

We pass now to the second question, concerning the relation between the New Testament apostolate and the subsequent episcopate. As we have seen, the letters of Ignatius show us monepiscopacy as a going concern in urban local churches in Asia Minor at the start of the second century, though we know nothing of the way they were appointed, or whether it involved a specific ordination to the episcopate or not. Nor, in fact, does it look as if monepiscopacy was universal at that time; in 1 Clement and the Didache, as in Acts 20. 28, Phil. 1.1, and the Pastorals, it appears that "presbyter" and "bishop" are correlative descriptions of the same persons. But monepiscopacy made its way throughout the Church, and we learn from Hippolytus, about A.D. 200, that it was by then the practice for each local bishop to be consecrated by bishops from other churches, while presbyters were ordained by the local bishop with other presbyters joining in the laying on of hands. These procedures accord with the usage instanced in the New Testament, as we saw, whereby oversight was given by those who themselves possessed it, and it is not possible to disprove, any more than to prove, the hypothesis that in parts of Christendom, at any rate, there was an unbroken line of commissioning from Apostles to bishops of the Ignatian sort running up to the third century, and from thence to the present day.

The important question, however, is not whether there was an unbroken succession of ordinations stemming from the Apostles throughout the Church, but what is the meaning of the development whereby within two centuries the single bishop, maintaining an episcopal succession in his own see, became (so far as we know) a universal Christian institution. The answer seems to be that the institution was shaped by the gospel itself—that is, by the once-for-all fact of Christ in history and the knowledge of Christ's continuing heavenly ministry which together form the substance of the Christian message. It was the pressure of gospel truth concerning Christ and his work that caused the Church to feel for the need for episcopal office once the uniquely comprehensive and authoritative oversight of the Apostles had ceased, and caused the development of the office to be accepted without demur (so far as we know) everywhere. The bishop, in idea, exhibits all the main continuing ministerial functions—all, that is, that were not personal to the

75

Apostles—concentrated in himself. As chief pastor of his diocese, whether defined as a single urban church with a multiple presbyterate or as the whole group of churches within a geographical area, he is the leader in preaching the gospel, safeguarding sound doctrine, teaching and governing the faithful, presiding at the Eucharist, and admitting to or excluding from communion. Fulfilling these apostolic ministries in Christ's name, he presents in his own person a small-scale image of the ministry of Christ himself, as it was in Galilee and as it is still, through his ministers, from his throne. The incarnation exemplified supremely both the *personal* principle, whereby God deals with men personally through a chosen person who represents him, and also the principle of *particularity*, whereby God deals with all men everywhere and at all times through one chosen person in whom space and time are transcended. Both these principles are reflected and embodied to a certain degree in all ordained ministers, but more fully in monepiscopacy than in other offices. Moreover, as president of the Eucharist and representative both of the universal Church to his own diocese and of his diocese to the universal Church, the bishop appears as a constitutive and focal element of the Church's visible oneness, just as Christ is the constitutive and focal element of that spiritual oneness which the Creed predicates of the Church, not by sight, but by faith. Finally, by his place in the episcopal succession and college, and by his regular ministry of transmitting Christ's commission in ordination, he exhibits the continuing identity and authenticity of the one Church of Christ in space and time.[1] Thus in idea, if not always in practice, the historic episcopate appears as an evangelical institution, witnessing by its structure in a specially clear and eloquent way to the continuing ministry of Christ in and to his Church. This is not to say that apart from episcopacy there can be no Church, or that ministers who were not episcopally commissioned

---

[1] It is extremely difficult to attach this theology of the episcopate to the English manifestation of the "suffragan bishop". He would seem to be a contingent historical product of a combination of over-large dioceses with the nineteenth-century concern to take confirmations seriously. The "bishop" who has special powers of ordaining and confirming, but no pastoral or governmental appointment integrated to the Church's structure, is a most potent cause of crude "pipe-line" thinking in relation to the episcopate. Our proposals in chs. 9 and 10 include a maximum size for a diocese which is calculated to obviate the need for suffragans and to prevent them arbitrarily reappearing on the scene (see pp. 138–9). For a discussion of the bishop in relation to the size of a diocese see below, p. 78.

at their ordination lack the authority and authorization of Christ. We are not asserting that at all. Our point is simply that the mon-episcopal idea exhibits the ministry of Christ with special fullness, and as such, once it has developed, it ought to be retained and valued. It is possible to deny that episcopacy rests on a necessity either of *being* or of *command* (the old distinction), and yet to hold that it is commended by necessity of *fitness*, the principle which determines means and methods in the light of a thing's nature, function, and purpose.

All this throws light in its turn on the problem of succession. One difficulty in discussing this subject is that we are all haunted by a view of apostolic succession which is mechanical and isolated from the Church's total life. Yet succession in some form is inseparable from the Church's life; thus, those Churches which interpret apostolic succession wholly in terms of preaching and maintaining apostolic truth substitute a succession of doctrine for a succession of bishops. The early Church laid stress on the succession of bishops in particular sees, as a guarantee of the authenticity of the version of Christian faith maintained there. There is in fact a vast differ-ence between a mechanical concept of succession, concerned only with the pedigree of ministers in isolation from the Church's organic life, and the scriptural pattern whereby, within that total organic life under Christ the Head, men are called and ordained to particular ministries, and so authorized by Christ to fulfil them, in order to enable the Church as a whole to keep faithful to Jesus' "flesh and blood" and obedient to his present authority as the risen and living Lord. To isolate episcopacy as something which can, so to speak, be injected into a Church without organic relation to its faith, liturgical practice, and pastoral structure is not only to reduce episcopacy to "gimmick" or mascot status, it is to empty it of its historic meaning and to invert its real purpose. Episcopacy is not an accolade bestowed on the Church as a finishing touch or a final decoration, nor is it a trifle of which a Church should make as little as possible, lest its members be offended. The historic episcopate—which, as such, must be sharply distinguished from the corrupt prelatical forms it has too often taken—is a pattern of apostolic pastoral ministry. It is not the visible Church's heart, nor the principle of its circulatory system, but (if the phrase is not over-bold) it is a part of the visible Church's developed bone-structure—no more, and no less; and the theological significance of successiveness in sees and orders is the same as the theological significance of successiveness in faithful belief, worship, and ordered life in the Church as a whole—again, no more, and no less. Succession, which means the deliberate practice of successiveness, is in all these spheres a standing visible witness to the fact that Jesus Christ, our living Lord and Head, is the same yesterday, today, and for ever, and that consequently his Church, and the commission and authority which ministers receive from him in his Church, are the same too.

How the apostolic ministry is exercised is of paramount importance. The acceptance of episcopacy must be implemented by providing those conditions in which it can fulfil its proper functions. In this respect the Church of England has nothing to boast about. The bishop, partly because of the size of dioceses and partly because of legal restrictions which shackle his pastoral office, has been isolated from the worshipping congregation. Seldom does he preside at the Eucharist. He thinks he does well if he visits each congregation once a year. Lack of time prevents him from exercising his teaching and expository office. He may write books, if he is a disciplined man, but he will have little opportunity of sitting with a congregation expounding the Word under the judgement of God. Perhaps, worst of all, he has not the time to exercise church discipline in a truly Christian way by bringing people to reconciliation in Christ. Inevitably, except in rare cases when he just has to make time to meet a P.C.C. or the vicar and churchwardens, he becomes a judge administering what must be very rough justice from a desk. In the selection of men for the ministry he has to fight to maintain his right to exercise his responsibility. In the appointment of men to parishes, he will, if he is patron, have real opportunity for consultation, but only too often he has to wait, with the churchwardens, who share his concern, hoping that the patrons will not just appoint "the next man on the list". As he contemplates synodical government, he wryly reflects the lack of trust which some of the provisions reflect and wonders if the true understanding and common obedience to God which must inspire it will ever break through. If, by contriving to spend a whole day in a parish from time to time, he seeks to remedy these defects, it will only serve, by its very effectiveness, to remind him how inadequately he is able to be a true bishop. Some are deeply distressed at our parody of episcopacy. Others, alas, appear to be satisfied with the mere fact that we have bishops, for why otherwise would they seek to inject episcopacy into a non-episcopal Church while remaining content for that Church's structure to be almost wholly unrelated to the episcopacy which it is taking into its system?

What then are the true functions of a bishop? First, with regard to pastoral care, he is the guardian of the preaching of the Word; this he must fulfil by his own teaching and study, by taking counsel with his presbyters and by teaching them, by taking counsel with his fellow bishops. In his liturgical ministry he gives sacramental expression to the headship of Christ over his Church. He who has the oversight ordains those who are called, and whose call is recognized by the faithful, to the ministry of oversight whereby they are empowered by the Spirit for the work of building up the Body of Christ. In his administrative and disciplinary care, he acts as a father seeking to bring the family of God into a unity of love and trust in which each bears the burdens of others.

As a bishop of the whole Church of God his office is the sacramental expression of the unity of Christians in time and in space. Above all his is a ministry of personal responsibility. He has to rule but "he is set to rule in the Church and with the Church rather than over the Church" (A. G. Hebert); he must not be an autocrat, but neither must he be a neutral chairman, voicing only the opinion of the majority to which he is subject. He fulfils his office as bishop by serving the Church, but it must be a service in which, obedient to the Word himself, he brings others to obedience, and not a service in which he is servile to those whom he seeks to serve.

So episcopacy must be capable of expression in every aspect of the Church's life. One bishop for each diocese must be the rule, if the bishop is to be seen as chief pastor of clergy and laity. A diocese must be of such a size as to have a representative synod, whose members can really know each other as well as represent the parishes. A diocese must be of such a size that the bishops can spend time with the clergy and laity, teaching, exhorting, rebuking, reconciling. The selection, training, and placing of men to share in the bishop's oversight must be shared with the whole People of God though the final responsibility is the bishop's alone. The bishop must be seen to be what he is in the liturgical life of the Church, the sacramental expression of the headship of Christ recalling all to the givenness of the Faith and to obedience under the Spirit to the living Lord.

If we really believe in episcopacy as part of the skeleton of the Church from which the presbyterate and diaconate derive, then what matters is to get the episcopate and its expression right. In the present divided state of Christendom it is, we believe, much preferable to get the episcopate right and then let other matters which derive from it fall into place, rather than to leave episcopacy all wrong or take it as a gimmick while being concerned with a technical validity of priest's orders. One reason why the proposed Anglican–Methodist Scheme was unsatisfactory was because it neither got episcopacy right nor got the validity of orders right. Many who opposed the Scheme were making two criticisms simultaneously and were saying, "If you are going to try and have a scheme aimed at validating orders, then you must do it in such a way that they are valid without question and this is just what the Scheme does not do", and also saying, "Validating orders without a restructuring on the basis of episcopacy and without agreeing on the doctrine of the ministry and Eucharist is a hollow process and not productive of true unity."

Not only must orders be related to episcopacy and not *vice versa*, but episcopacy must be related to organic unity. As two of us have argued elsewhere,[1] intercommunion which does not reflect a unity capable of visible expression is not true to the New Testament teaching on unity. We would also argue that intercommunion based on the acceptance of some technicality of orders, without its implementation in a unity of belief or practice, is equally open to objection.

QUESTION 3: EPISCOPAL AND NON-EPISCOPAL MINISTRIES

What we have written about episcopacy clearly raises the question of non-episcopal orders. We would make two basic points:

(a) If a Christian community is regarded as having an ecclesial character, it is impossible simply to regard those in non-episcopal orders as laymen. This is not just a question of courtesy but is one of theology, as is recognized in the decree on Ecumenism of Vatican II.

[1] In the article by Colin Buchanan and the Bishop of Willesden; *Theology* (October 1969), reprinted as Appendix 3, pp. 176–86.

(b) Nevertheless a single non-episcopal order cannot be directly equated with any one of the three orders of bishops, presbyters, and deacons. The distinction between them is not ordination, in the sense of being solemnly set apart by a Christian community. The distinction is essentially one of relationship to a bishop and thereby to the Universal Church. It is, in many cases, also a distinction of the theological understanding and interpretation of the ministry. It is for this reason that we say that we must first get our theology of the ministry right and then integrate the ministries as part of a move into organic unity by relating the existing ministries to the bishop who is the focal point of that organic unity. Having said that, we wish to quote a remarkable discussion of the relationship between episcopal and non-episcopal ministries by Fr David N. Power, O.M.I., in his recent book:[1]

It is impossible to go fully into the question but it may here be suggested that the responsibility of spiritual leadership, and the position of representing Christ as head of his church, may in extraordinary circumstances come from some source other than ordination through the laying-on of hands, or through the laying-on of hands even when the succession from the apostles has been broken. We have already seen that historical evidence from the New Testament and the early church suggests that there may well be no absolutely exclusive link between the laying-on of hands and the sacred ministry, even the ministry of the eucharist. Office and pastoral ministry, we said, are not just the result of the transmission of powers and authority from the apostles. They depend as much on the Spirit, and arise within the community of believers and for the community. Where in some extraordinary circumstances a community may be left without pastors, the Spirit may intervene to give the charism of spiritual leadership, so that within the community itself the person concerned is recognized as its head and acknowledged also as representative of Christ and minister in his name of the eucharist.

Likewise, where there is schism and, through the fault as much of the parent body as of the group which breaks away, christian communities live apart, so that there is a break in the laying-on of hands, the new community, because it is a

[1] *Ministers of Christ and His Church* (Chapman 1969). The quotation is from pp. 177–8.

community which believes in Christ as Lord, is not left without the Spirit. The laying on of hands may then be reintroduced into this community as a way of acknowledging those to whom the Spirit gives the grace of the ministry and as the expression of the desire to maintain continuity with the apostolic church, despite the inevitable schism. In both cases mentioned, there is a responsibility communicated through the grace of the Spirit, and because there is this responsibility which places the recipient in a particular position within the community there is also a legitimate ministry.

To accept this hypothesis is not to take away from the importance and significance of ordination through the laying-on of hands, within the line of apostolic succession of the ministry. It is necessary to show the continuity of the church with the apostolic church, and to signify full church communion. We are speaking only of extraordinary conditions under which, despite the deficiencies of the sacramental sign, a legitimate ministry may exist. We have insisted that the functions of the ministry belong to a responsible position within the community of believers, and that the power to posit ministerial acts is not to be understood as a physical power. It belongs to whomsoever is manifestly in the position of representing Christ in this community, because of the place which he occupies in it and because he is accepted as such by the community. It would seem possible that this position be given to somebody through means other than the laying-on of hands within the line of strict apostolic succession. Consequently it would also seem possible to admit the existence of a genuine God-given ministry in the church, allowing the exercise of all the functions proper to the pastoral ministry, which is not transmitted in this way. At the same time we must affirm that this kind of ordination is required for the more fitting transmission of the ministry, and ought to be retained or reintroduced in all circumstances where this is possible.[1] The sign, of course, would be deficient, and to some extent also the effect signified. This would not, however, destroy the total reality of

---

[1] We would never agree to speak of a layman as a layman celebrating and consecrating the eucharist. There could, however, be circumstances where a Christian might act as minister of Christ only *per modum actus*. [Footnote and italics Power's.]

the act of appointment or of the acts posited by the pastor. What would be lacking in the reality would be precisely that which is lacking in the sign, namely, full ecclesial communion.[1]

"CHARACTER" AND ORDINATION FOR LIFE

In conclusion, we must say something about what in traditional Catholic terminology is called "indelible character". The concept is reflected in the revised Canons of the Church of England. Canon C 1 (2) says, "No person who has been admitted to the order of bishop, priest, or deacon can ever be divested of the character of his order..." Some today react strongly against what has come to be regarded as an essentially juridical conception. It is true that the question of character arises most frequently in a juridical context, when it has to be determined whether a man can still function legally or canonically as a minister or whether he is still subject to the restrictions of clerical status. Nevertheless, there lie behind the concept fundamental implications of the gospel which must not be ignored: namely, the irrevocable nature of Christian commitment in response to the call of God, the faithfulness of Christ as Head of his Church, and the relationship between Christian discipleship and a man's personality.

In discussion of character, emphasis is often laid upon the fact that, while the ministry is a profession, a means of earning one's living, it is, because of the very nature of the profession, one in which there can be no distinction between the priest's personal life and his professional life in terms of Christian discipleship. He stakes his livelihood upon the fact that he is a Christian.

While such emphasis embodies an important element of Christian truth it puts too much stress upon the fact that being a priest involves earning one's living by it. If the argument about character is made to rest upon the fact of full-time paid service it may be properly answered that the office of bishop or presbyter is not *necessarily* full-time or paid and at times in the Church has not been so.[2]

---

[1] Cf. also E. Schillebeeckx, o.p., "Catholic Understanding of Office", in *Theological Studies*, xxx. 4 (December 1969), pp. 567 ff. [our footnote].

[2] The excellent discussion of character in Leslie Houlden's essay on Priesthood in the Preparatory Essays for Lambeth (*Lambeth Essays on Ministry*, edited by the Archbishop of Canterbury (S.P.C.K. 1969), pp. 39–51) is somewhat weakened by the fact that he makes too much of a priest being full-time.

The first point to be made is that, in the case of an ordained man, his public acts as well as his private acts are *ipso facto* professedly Christian acts. His Christian commitment is inextricably interwoven with his public functions as liturgical president, guardian of the Word, or Shepherd of the flock. He cannot *qua* Christian act as a private person.

If, however, it were merely a question of the public nature of his life, it would be possible for him to withdraw into a lay Christian discipleship. But if, above all, the ministry is the sacramental expression of the continuing headship of Christ over his Church, and if it is the function of the ordained man, whether bishop or presbyter, to witness to the utter faithfulness of Christ to his Church and to those whom he has called, the irrevocable nature of the ordained man's calling is clear. If he abandons that calling he will witness to the frailty of human nature. In so far as he remains the sacramental expression of Christ's headship he witnesses to the fact that Christ will not fail his flock, though men may fail him. The irrevocable nature of the ministry is a standing reminder to all Christians that a Christian can never become a pagan; he can only become an apostate.

The assertion of character is therefore an assertion, first, of the consistency of Christ, and, secondly, of the power of the Holy Spirit.

FURTHER NOTES

I: LAY ELDERSHIP

One different pattern of ministry which must attract attention, simply because it has four centuries of history behind it, is the Presbyterian distinction between preaching (i.e. ministerial) and ruling (i.e. lay) elders. This derives rather problematically from I Tim. 5.17, whence it could be inferred that there are presbyters who preach and teach and presbyters who do not. In the event this system, as far as we have encountered it, seems to involve a confusion of language leading to a far more important contradiction of ideas. As a matter of language, the word "lay" is usually reserved for those who are not ordained—but "ruling" elders, like preaching elders, are ordained for life. This would suggest they might be dubbed "lay" or "elders", but not both at once. And if we press the question, then the allocation of these men to one category or another brings out the contradiction of ideas. If these elders are ordained ministers in the usual sense, then although the ordained ministry is not now reserved to those who are professionally employed in it, nevertheless there remain no lay ministries in the Church at all, and ordination has lost much of its pastoral, liturgical, and sacramental aspects. On the other hand, if they are really laymen, then their appointment for life precludes in advance a proper sharing of differing functions amongst the members of the body. The hierarchical and juridical concepts of the Church have then invaded the field of the laity as well as that of the clergy, and the result is still to strip the ordinary layman of any functions in the Church except purely passive ones.

It has been suggested in our group that the institution of ruling elders was a product of first groping steps towards a lay maturity. In pragmatic terms it was thus an understandable and even commendable result of the Reformation, but it belongs to its times. We see little place for it in the ordering of church life in the twentieth century, where a greater lay maturity is one of the terms of the problem.

2: PRESBYTER OR PRIEST

Two of the authors of this book were critical of the proposed use of "presbyter" in the Scheme for Anglican–Methodist Unity. Some explanation is due, therefore, of the fact that in this book we all use "presbyter" as the norm, though we also use the word "priest". Those who objected to its use in the Scheme admitted quite openly that "presbyter" was technically a correct term to use to describe the second of the holy orders and were, of course, aware that both "priest" and "presbyter" are derived from the same word *presbuteros*. Their objection was based upon the context in which the proposed use was set—a context provided as much by the Service of Reconciliation, the statements about ministry, and the manner in which episcopacy was proposed to be exercised in Stage One as by the Preface to the New Ordinal. In this book, however, we have been concerned to discuss ministry in terms of the primary minister, the bishop, and to relate to him the office and function of the second order. Since the special function of the word "presbyter" is to distinguish the minister of the second order from the minister of the first, i.e. the bishop, we believe it is right to use it. We have also sought to set our discussion of the ministry in the context of the whole gospel and in particular of the doctrines of tradition, justification, the Church, and the sacraments, including the eucharistic sacrifice. We believe that the discussion above has sufficiently secured those doctrinal points, agreement on which must precede any acceptance of the word "presbyter" as an alternative to "priest". We have not abandoned its use, as is apparent from the book as a whole, and regard it as a possible alternative at the very least, because an ordained man does not cease to be a member of the royal priesthood of the Church. Since, however, our concern has been to relate the bishop to gospel and to Church, and the priest to the bishop, we believe it right to use the term which expresses that very relationship.

3: LAY CELEBRATION

The Church can only function as the Church if it is dependent upon Christ as the eternal High Priest and Shepherd of the flock. While an individual Christian, has, of course, access to God it is only by virtue of his incorporation into Christ and his membership of the Spirit-filled Body. This is particularly evident when he takes part in the Eucharist. It is the Supper of the Lord, who is the Head of the Church, his Body, and is himself its Saviour. The Church is so structured by the gospel as to give continuing sacramental expression to this fact. A man is ordained in order that, as a bishop or as the deputy of the bishop, he may proclaim in his own person, as representative of Christ and minister in his name, his headship over the Church.

We would agree with Father Power, as quoted above (p. 82), that in some extraordinary circumstance, such as the oft-quoted desert-island situation, it would be the duty of a group of Christians to appoint one to minister in Christ's name, rather than fail to obey the Lord's command to break the bread. But following the gospel principle we have outlined above, we must say that such action presupposes that there must be a minister and does not justify the notion that any layman can celebrate, which does not accord with those principles. Further, though the position of a person so appointed would be anomalous, he would cease to be a layman. He would be, for those particular circumstances, the person in whom the headship of Christ was embodied and expressed.

However this may be, we have to ask ourselves what sort of

rules would most appropriately express our sacramental theology in a future united Church. The thrust of the last two chapters should make it clear that we would envisage that such rules would have to confine the celebration of the Eucharist to the bishop or presbyter. If exceptional cases arise people in them must judge for themselves, but we think it impossible to embody such exceptional cases in the rules.

4: THE ORDINATION OF WOMEN

The Dean of York, Dr Alan Richardson, in his recent discussion of the ordination of women,[1] virtually says that there is only one serious theological issue involved, namely the right of any one branch of the historic Church to determine the issue. He points out that it raises the question of authority in the separated branches of the Universal Church of Christ and goes much deeper than discussion about whether such unilateral action would help or hinder progress towards organic unity amongst the Churches. He then passes to what he describes as pastoral considerations, among which he includes the question of whether a woman instituted as rector or vicar of a parish could be the head of the family in the same way that Christ is head of the Church. He asserts that she could not be the representative *persona* or at least not in the same sense as a man can be.

He contents himself with two assertions, namely that the arguments are inconclusive and that the pastorate of a woman parish priest would be different from that of a man.

We agree with what the Dean says about the importance of the question of authority. We should, however, maintain that what he describes as pastoral considerations raise very important theological issues concerning the nature and function of the ministry and the differing functions performed by members of the one Body (Rom. 12. 4; I Cor. 12. 4–31).

Two points seem clear to us. First, for both reasons given by the Dean, any unilateral action would precipitate questions of the authority of separate Churches. Secondly, much more serious consideration must be given to it on the basis of what is demanded by the gospel and its implications. Sociological considerations,

---

[1] *Lambeth Essays on Ministry*, pp. 75–8.

psychological considerations, and the like have to be taken into account, but in the last resort it is the gospel which must shape and determine the decisions of the Church and not contemporary ideas. For these reasons, the issue cannot be ignored or treated as of secondary importance, when schemes of union are under consideration.

For the moment, however, we can neither quickly resolve the issue nor delay questions of reunion to wait upon such resolution. We have therefore found it not only possible but also desirable to find a way ahead which opens the door to multilateral reunion, does not depend upon existing denominations renouncing their existing practice, and yet neither accepts women in the episcopate or presbyterate at the point of inauguration, nor provides for their ordination in the united Church.[1]

---

[1] The treatment of this question in the context of our outline plan for reunion is to be found in ch. 10 on p. 141.

PART TWO

Joining the Structure

"Jesus Christ ... in whom the whole structure is fitly joined
together."

Ephesians 2. 20-1

This second part of the book picks up three great issues which
arise as general principles in the quest for reunion today. The
solutions we offer to these are far more closely related to the particular times and place in which we write than are the contents of
the foregoing chapters. They are, however, more strictly approaches
towards a scheme rather than the outline of a scheme.

5

Uniformity and Pluriformity

CONTAINING AND SUBDUING

In 1967 the late Professor Ian Henderson of Glasgow published *Power without Glory*, a trenchant indictment of the modern Anglican insistence on episcopacy in united Churches as arrogant and imperialistic. In the course of a discussion of issues Henderson raised, entitled "Is Ecumenism a Power Game?", Professor D. M. MacKinnon wrote as follows:

> ...the Church of England, and indeed the Anglican Communion, is a deeply divided Church. The term "comprehensiveness" may be used sometimes not to advertise a source of strength, but to disguise and conceal deep undercurrents of profound, even passionate, disagreement. Initially, within the Church of England this comprehensiveness was secured by the Elizabethan Settlement, which sought through the intervention of the executive to secure a real conformity at the level of religious practice, coupled with a measure of genuine freedom at the level of intellectual opinion. *Always at some point the Anglican Communion reveals itself even today as still in bondage to the belief that some such imposed settlement can contain and subdue through enforced adoption of agreed forms of worship (including here the so-called inauguration services of uniting Churches) the stresses and strains of deeply opposed theological convictions.*[1]

The sentence in italics is the starting-point for the argument of this chapter. We have three agreements with Professor MacKinnon to record and develop.

First, we agree that comprehensiveness, in MacKinnon's sense of an imposed settlement of a uniform practice designed to "contain and subdue" the clash of opposing principles, is a source, not of strength, but of unreality and weakness. To start with, where the clash of principles concerns matters of prime

[1] *The Stripping of the Altars* (Collins 1969), p. 78; our italics.

importance, a uniformity of practice seemingly meant to conceal the divisions and divert attention from them must look like a gesture of doctrinal levity and indifferentism. (Ambiguous doctrinal formulations with the same apparent purpose will inevitably have the same look, and be open to the same criticism.) It has to be said that the Anglican image has suffered disastrously in modern times from well-meant apologias which, in face of existing theological division within the Church, treat the uniformity of the 1662 Prayer Book as determining the nature of Anglicanism more decisively than theology does. If this were really so, then all those Roman Catholics who insist so disturbingly that doctrinal latitudinarianism is basic to the Anglican position would be right. But is it so? The history of the Reformation in England, and of Anglican theological work in the seventeenth century, hardly suggests it; and if the appeal is to more recent times, it must be pointed out that what has actually gone on in the cockpit of Anglicanism since the appearance of the *Tracts for the Times* (1833-40) and *Essays and Reviews* (1860) rang up the curtain on its modern era has been a three-cornered theological struggle between different shades of "High", "Low", and "Broad", in which it has become plain that at some points (not, of course, always the same points!) all three bodies of opinion find 1662 uniformity to be a shoe that pinches quite sharply. The "average Anglican", the devotee of 1662 whose faith is sustained by a sense of history and a feeling for institutions rather than by theological conviction, and who stands halfway between all extremes of opinion, was always, like the "average man", something of an abstraction, and, if anyone answering to this description was found today, he would have to be described as a bird no less old-fashioned than rare. It is not in fact possible to give a realistic account of the dynamics of modern Anglicanism if one starts from, or ends with, an agreed uniformity of practice, whether that of 1662 or some other, as an ultimate Anglican fact. Issues in current debate—the relation between episcopacy, valid orders, and inter-communion, for instance, or the doctrine of God, the world, and the meaning of worship—challenge the ideal of uniformity, as well as our actual present uniformity, such as it is, at a profounder level than that at which these things were challenged by the Puritans during the century following the Elizabethan settlement. Any new uniformity which seemed designed simply to "contain and subdue" differences such as these, which touch primary matters of faith, would inevitably prove a source of new division and revolt; for the sense that the Church is trying to evade an issue on which a man believes he has vital truth which the whole Church should obey will prompt him to shout all the louder about it, and to press the issue all the harder. The debates which grew up around the Service of Reconciliation between 1963 and 1969 are a clear case in point, and, if the Service was resurrected, it would certainly become an engine of division once more.

Secondly, we agree that to be wedded to the idea that liturgical uniformity can "contain and subdue" the sort of theological tensions by which modern Anglicanism is agitated is "bondage" indeed. Theologically and psychologically, the idea is unplausible. Imposed liturgical uniformity is not found in the New Testament; Scripture nowhere suggests that those who are one in Christ should necessarily express this by all using exactly the same words in their main acts of worship. As for later history, there is no doubt that the Tudor monarchs who introduced England to uniformity valued it no less (probably, indeed, more) as a means to political and social solidarity than as a means of deepening spiritual unity. To assume that now, four hundred years on, in a post-Christian political *milieu*, and in face of current debates about God and the Church, the imposing of common liturgical forms, accommodating all views, is the right and only way to spiritual solidarity, is both naive and forlorn. Clearly, this uncriticized assumption from the past is a rut in which many are still stuck; but the fact is, as we have said, that in a situation like ours, in which debates about order are felt to reflect actual differences of faith, the imposing of liturgical forms which deliberately evade the issue can only deepen division by its irritant effect on those who believe that the Church ought to heed the witness which they bear on one side or the other. To feel obliged nonetheless, as a loyal Anglican, to back a "uniformity" policy, and to set one's face against any other kind of solution, when faced with problems like these, is really a rather pathetic traditionalism, objectionably pragmatic in principle and doomed to ineffectiveness in practice.

Thirdly, we agree that the "so-called inauguration services of uniting Churches" are cases in point, and we include the Anglican–Methodist Service of Reconciliation with these. This Service was, and was defended in the Report as, an attempt to "contain and subdue" by means of liturgical uniformity a supposed theological polarization concerning the Christian ministry. On the basis of a demonstration that the wording of the Service could be squared with either of the competing extremes, Anglicans and Methodists were asked to accept it as a basis for the future fellowship of their Churches in intercommunion and ultimately union. The result, though it surprised some, was entirely predictable. Those for whom Anglicanism on the one hand, and Methodism on the other, were first and foremost positions of theological principle, and not just forms of ecclesiastical culture, opposed the proposal tooth and nail on the ground that it threatened their Church's integrity. By their reactions to the Service of Reconciliation, it might have been said, you shall know them—how far they understood their church-manship in theological terms, as a matter of confessing and obeying revealed truth, or how far they fell short of doing this. In fact, the voting at every level in the Church of England showed that too many Anglicans felt that the Service lacked the integrity which full communion requires for it to be a viable option.

The debate on the Service started from the defence of it that the Report gave, and the polarization which it posited was taken as a fixed point. This made it appear that the Service was being rejected by different people for precisely opposite reasons. Some, so it seemed, were against it because it was too much like an ordination for Methodist ministers, and some because it was too little like one. The complaint of some was apparently that it did not express fully enough a pipeline theory of orders and an exclusive correlation between episcopacy and intercommunion, and the complaint of others seemed to be that it gave too clear an expression to these principles, which were anathematized as a fable and an occasion of sin respectively. The manoeuvres of the debate convinced many that the Service, vulnerable to criticism though it was, ought still to be accepted on the grounds that it was the only possible way forward, it being obviously impossible for its critics ever to agree on an alternative! And when the present writers let it be known that they were attempting to produce an alternative, friend and foe alike made no secret of their scepticism. The following chapters, however, do in fact propose an alternative which we all believe to be fully practicable, and which, from our varied theological stand-points, we are all ready to justify as obedience to God's revealed truth in the matter of church union in England. On what basis, it will be asked, are these proposals made? How has it been possible for

"Catholics" and "Evangelicals" like ourselves to agree positively on a course of action? Is this an ecumenical conjuring trick? or what? It will be worth devoting a few paragraphs to answering these questions, so preparing our readers' minds for what is to come.

AGREEING WITHOUT COERCING

Our basis for making common proposals is not far to seek. It lies in the doctrinal agreements spelt out in the previous chapters. The previous scheme, being institutionally rather than theologically orientated, did not probe deeply enough to strike the oil of a genuine theological consensus, and for lack of this was obliged to pin all its hopes on contrived uniformity and pragmatic administrative adjustment—an insufficient basis, as has now appeared. We have tried to go deeper, and believe ourselves to have established a doctrinal consensus which, though not *complete* (for we still have our differences, and see many areas where Catholics and Evangelicals need to continue to debate), is yet *sufficient* to open up for us a road to a united Church, a road each step along which will be an example of "doing the truth". In our doctrinal discussions, we tried to use our variant heritages as Anglicans constructively rather than centrifugally, and instead of digging into entrenched positions from which we then agree to differ we have laid together foundations which will bear the weight of the practical programme we are now to erect upon them. We do not attempt to "contain and subdue" supposedly ultimate doctrinal cleavages by means of equivocal liturgical uniformity. Instead, having shown (as we believe) that the doctrinal cleavages of the Report are not so ultimate as is sometimes supposed, we now call, on the basis of our proclaimed theological uniformity, for a readiness frankly to accept pluriformity in the realm of order as a theologically justifiable state of affairs when the Churches of England are on the road to union, starting from where they are. Our theological uniformity is unambiguous in its positive affirmations and accepted goals, and this enables us to accept, in the course of readjustment, temporary anomalies on which it would be hard to agree in any other context. We believe that the course proposed in the following chapters is sounder and more hopeful than the incoherent uniformitarian pragmatism of the Service of Reconciliation,[1] predicated as it was on

---

[1] See "A Bog of Illogic", Appendix 5, pp. 193–201.

agreement to differ about major questions concerning Scripture and Tradition, the Church, the ministry, and the Eucharist.

Not that we are against all uniformity. As the previous paragraph has shown, we are very much for uniformity in the realm of doctrine and goals. This is an aspect of the uniformity which the New Testament requires—the uniformity of one heart and mind, one spirit of worship, and one sense of mission; the inward uniformity that results from a common knowledge of one Father, one Saviour, and one Holy Spirit. External uniformity, which, as was said, is not found in the New Testament, can be justified only to the extent that it promotes and safeguards this inward solidarity of God's people. From this standpoint, liturgical and disciplinary uniformity has been valued in the past, and rightly so. Reformation divines were not wrong to justify Tudor uniformity as a genuine sign and expression of unity, and as a pastoral boon, making for peace, spiritual harmony, and edification in the Church. The justification was valid, because the liturgy and discipline in question were good and godly. But uniformity can be the opposite of a blessing. There is a spontaneous pluriformity in the manifestation of the Spirit, as Rom. 12 and 1 Cor. 12 (to look no further) show, and a too tight uniformity will quench this. Full conscientious obedience to known truth is required of all Christians, and uniformity is indefensible where it inhibits this and so causes consciences to be offended. Also, a tradition of uniformity tends to breed the twin evils of institutionalism and triumphalism in churchmen's minds. The Church of England has had experience of all these unhappy things, and the institutionalist–triumphalist syndrome has been perhaps the worst of all. We cannot be proud of the way in which in the past reasons of theology have been sought and found to justify accidents of history such as the passing of the royalist Act of Uniformity of 1662; or the way in which some have affirmed that God gives less grace to non-episcopal Churches, or non-liturgical Churches, or Churches lacking a "professional" ministry, or Churches whose communion discipline has not commended itself as strict enough; or the recurring argument that the Free Churches suffer from a Donatist infection, which can only be cured by capitulation and return to the Establishment. Nor can we do other than regret the way in which the continuity of institutional practice, rather than of the ministry of the Lord Christ, is repeatedly held up as the principle of the Church's identity and being, with, of course, adverse implications for late arrivals on the ecclesiastical scene. In saying this, we are not of course denying that the institutions of baptism, the Eucharist, and the ministry are part of the given essence of Church life, in every age, but we are affirming as strongly as we can that institutionalism—the deifying, or rather idolizing, of the particular form that these institutions took in some particular age— is a dangerous and demonic perversion. The distinction between institutions which as such belong to the given uniformity of essential Christianity, and their historically conditioned outward forms, which as such are always to some extent negotiable and in need of reform, may be hard to draw, but it is vital that we should learn to draw it.

The conclusion to which these reflections tend is as follows. When exploring the question of union with non-episcopal Churches, the Church of England should ask *not*, in the first instance, what do they lack as compared with us that we can give them, or what do we lack as compared with them that we can receive from them (these are questions about our historic institutional forms, with triumphalist overtones, and we should not start there), *but* we should raise with them the three questions that follow:

(i) How far, in terms both of historic corporate profession and present states of mind, do we exhibit theological uniformity with them, and they with us, in a way that we can all recognize as scriptural?

(ii) How far can we achieve theological uniformity in determining common ecclesial goals for the united Church which we seek?

(iii) How far can we achieve theological uniformity in categorizing present disparities between us as non-essential matters, or else, if they appear to touch issues of greater importance, how far can we achieve theological uniformity in planning for their reduction and elimination?

Then, if the answers to these questions are satisfactory, it becomes possible to justify the temporary anomalies of a pluriform practice on the road to union; which is the method we pursue in the subsequent chapters of this book.

6

Confessing the Faith

The Christian gospel is the good news that God has brought salvation to the world by sending his Son Jesus Christ to be the Saviour of mankind. "The Lord God of Israel has visited and redeemed his people, and has raised up a horn of salvation for us in the house of his Servant David" (Luke 1. 68–9). This salvation, prefigured and foreseen in the old Israel as the event towards which all its long history was converging, is now offered in and by the Church which is the new Israel, to all men everywhere. "In Christ Jesus [the Gentiles] who once were far off have been brought near in the blood of Christ", who "came and preached peace to you who were far off and peace to those who were near" (Eph. 2. 13,17). The salvation which the gospel sets forth is laid hold of by faith, and its fruits are manifested in the life of faith and fellowship lived by the Church, the Spirit-filled body of Christ. But precisely because the gospel is *news*, its acceptance by faith involves the activity of both the will and the intellect, difficult as it may be to specify the way in which these two faculties of the soul are related to each other and to the grace of God. Believing *in* includes believing *that*; I cannot believe in Christ, in the New Testament sense, without believing that God has wrought salvation through him and that he is himself the Saviour.

It is therefore not surprising that in the New Testament some profession of belief is the natural, and presumably invariable, preliminary to, and condition for, baptism. The burden of the confession was belief in the divine Lordship of Jesus of Nazareth, identified as the Christ (the Saviour-King of God's people). The speech of Peter on the day of Pentecost, which led to the baptism of three thousand people, reached its climax in the declaration that "God has made him both Lord and Christ, this Jesus whom you crucified", and it was on the strength of this declaration that baptism was both offered and welcomed. The preparation of the Ethiopian eunuch was brief and concentrated but, if the Western text of

Acts is to be relied on, his baptism was prefaced by the confession "I believe that Jesus Christ is the Son of God". Even those who reject this as an interpolation must admit that it reflects the practice of the primitive Church. The Philippian jailer, whose preparation must have been equally sketchy, was told, "Believe in the Lord Jesus and you will be saved, you and your whole household", and it was only when they had been instructed in the implications of this demand that baptism was conferred upon them. Scholars have debated whether the primordial baptismal formula was "in the name of Jesus Christ" or "in the name of the Father, Son, and Holy Spirit". The last verse but one of St Matthew's Gospel—and here at least the textual evidence is unanimous—traces the trinitarian formula back to Christ himself. In any case, baptismal profession of faith in Christ and entry by baptism into the Spirit-filled Church necessarily raises the question of the relations between the three Persons. The unselfconscious manner in which St Paul, in the greetings with which his letters open, associates Jesus with the Father in a way which by any Jewish precedent would have appeared as shocking blasphemy (e.g. "Grace to you and peace from God the Father and the Lord Jesus Christ" (1 Cor. 1. 3)), to say nothing of the trinitarian prayer at the end of 2 Corinthians ("The grace of the Lord Jesus Christ and the love of God and the fellowship of the Holy Spirit be with you all" (13.14)) makes it plain that, in however undeveloped a form, a definite doctrinal commitment, explicitly christological, implicitly trinitarian, was at the heart of the life of the primitive Christian community.[1]

Not that the New Testament Christians had standardized verbal forms for expressing their theological commitments. It seems clear that they did not; even for the solemnities of baptism and the Eucharist the verbal forms varied. But this should not cause surprise. Standard forms of words could not, in the nature of the case, establish themselves till the Church was past its first generation, and traditions of teaching and liturgy had settled down. It is true that behind New Testament phraseology lies the common linguistic heritage of the Septuagint; but the thoughts with which Christians were grappling, more or less consciously, from the start—such thoughts as the plurality-in-unity of God, the divine humanity of Jesus, the eschatological complex of "now" and "not yet" in the divine saving work—were thoughts which no human mind had

[1] Cf. A. W. Wainwright, *The Trinity in the New Testament* (S.P.C.K. 1962).

hitherto come remotely near, and the effort to grasp and state them took the New Testament theologians beyond familiar Septuagint usage into realms of total verbal novelty. From one point of view the New Testament theology appears as a series of major linguistic experiments, radically redeploying existing verbal resources in order to set forth "what no eye has seen, nor ear heard, nor the heart of man conceived...the depths of God" (1 Cor. 2. 9–10, R.S.V.). The uniform success of these experiments, which is so complete as to defy explanation save in terms of Paul's claim that "we impart this in words...taught by the Spirit" (v. 13), must not be allowed to hide from us how extraordinarily bold they were.

But some describe the variety of New Testament *idioms* as a variety of *theologies*. This, however, is a major blunder. Words must be distinguished from thoughts, or rather, in this case, from things thought about; and verbal variation, or fluidity of language, must not be equated with divergence of views or ideas. Complementary concepts and identical views are perfectly consistent with differences, even polarized differences, in the use of words. (Think of Paul and James!) In fact, it has often been shown, both in small books like A. M. Hunter's *The Unity of the New Testament* and in large ones like Alan Richardson's *Introduction to the Theology of the New Testament*, that what lies behind the linguistic pluriformity of the New Testament is a single consistent way of thinking about the work of God in Christ, on the one hand, and the meaning of Christian faith, hope, love, and good works on the other. Individual writers develop different aspects of it, and with different emphases, but the faith of the New Testament first to last is one thing, with a central content that remains the same. The theological homogeneity which, as contextual exegesis shows, underlies its linguistic diversity goes back to the earliest strata of material, and there is no reason to doubt that it was there from the very first.

HISTORIC CONFESSIONS

From the primitive New Testament expressions of belief, focused in baptismal confessions, the Catholic Creeds developed. Their trinitarian shape witnesses to this. The so-called Athanasian Creed is an exception, for, whatever its origin, it was certainly not a baptismal profession; but both the "Apostles'" and the "Nicene"

Creeds, as well as the host of other creeds with which the early Church abounded, are elaborations and clarifications of baptismal professions. The new Christian was to be baptized in the name of the three divine Persons and therefore he professed faith in the three divine Persons. Indeed it appears from the *Apostolic Tradition* that around the year 200 at Rome (or wherever that intriguing document had its origin) the candidate made his profession in the course of the actual baptism, the threefold profession of faith being dovetailed into the threefold pouring of the water; and some scholars hold that no words were spoken at all by the baptizing minister at this point of the rite, the candidate's own profession constituting what later theology would describe as the "form" of the sacrament. And it is highly significant that when, in the fourth and fifth centuries, in the course of the Arian and christological controversies, it was felt necessary to impose credal formulas as tests of orthodoxy, the formulas to which conciliar authority was given were in fact elaborations and clarifications of baptismal professions. This is clear, whatever may be the precise history behind the creed of Nicaea and the Constantinopolitan creed (which we miscall "Nicene"), and the connection (or non-connection) of the latter with the Council of Constantinople of A.D. 381. The implication is that heresy consists in unfaithfulness on the part of the heretic to the faith in which he was baptized. The intimate relation between faith and baptism, and between faith and membership of the Church, could not be more evident.

The Reformation in the West produced a number of "confessions", by means of which the national Churches which split off from the Roman allegiance sought to identify themselves in a warring Christendom as authentic local expressions of the one Church of Christ. These confessions, of which the Thirty-nine Articles are one, were not ecumenical gestures of unity, but local responses to a situation of ecclesiastical crisis and division. Their background was not baptismal profession but ecclesiastical politics and polemics, and they contain a great mass of local, occasional, and controversial matter which has no counterpart in the creeds. Nonetheless, they do not differ from the creeds in character and intention as much as is sometimes made out. On the one hand, the patristic creeds are like the later confessions in having their own anti-heretical ecclesiastical slant and function. It is not hard to trace the influence of the conflict with Gnosticism in determining the stress of the "Apostles'" Creed on the facts of creation and incarnation, and the "Nicene" Creed makes a point of including a particular theological development from its own age (the *homoousion*) directed against a current heresy (Arianism) which was felt to threaten the Church's identity as "the pillar and bulwark of the truth" (1 Tim. 3. 15, R.S.V.). On the other hand, the Reformation confessions are like the ecumenical creeds in their concern to clarify and fence around the essentials of New Testament faith, to which the original baptismal profession had looked.

Gustaf Aulén, in his book *Reformation and Catholicity*, argues powerfully that the apostolic, patristic, and Reformation confessions are in direct line, the two latter seeking successfully, against different backgrounds of debate, to safeguard the substance of the former. The New Testament confession of Jesus as Lord and Christ had four focal points: first, the fact that the man Jesus has risen, and lives and reigns; second, the fact that he died for sins on the cross; third, the fact that he will come again, for the final salvation of his people; fourth, the fact that he is God the Son, co-creator with his Father. The two patristic creeds, centring upon the thought of Jesus as God incarnate and so as divine Saviour, re-affirmed these four points, guarding them against docetism and Arianism respectively. The Reformation confession of Jesus as the one in and through whom sinners are justified by faith alone and saved by sovereign grace was an elucidation and defence of the same apostolic confession, this time against a semi-Pelagian doctrine of salvation by meritorious churchmanship. In substance and purpose, Aulén maintains, the three confessions are at one.

Aulén's contention is demonstrably true of the Thirty-nine Articles, which began by recapitulating the witness of the creeds to the Godhead and the incarnation (Articles 1–5), and by approving the creeds *in toto* as biblical (8). Hereby they show that their purpose is to cleave to the faith of the creeds, and to preclude any lapses from it, and that the further doctrinal determinations which they offer are supplementary to the creeds, not contradictory of them. From this, the Articles proceed, in B. J. Kidd's words, to "expend most of their energy in anthropology. They deal with Sin, Faith, Works, Justification, and the Means of Grace"[1]—matters which the creeds had barely mentioned. It is their positive statements on these

---

[1] *The Thirty-nine Articles*, p. 4.

matters, more than anything else, that gives the Articles their abiding worth and importance. Aulén limited his study of the post-patristic period to the Church of the West, but a review of the later statements of the Eastern Church (e.g. that of the Synod of Bethlehem) would certainly lead to a parallel conclusion about solidarity with the faith of the Fathers and the Scriptures.

CONSERVING THE CHURCH'S CONFESSION

The truth to which the facts so far reviewed alert us is that the Church, as the appointed guardian and trustee of the apostolic deposit, and thus "the pillar and bulwark of the truth", has a constant duty to confess and hold fast "the faith once for all delivered to the saints" (Jude 3). No claim to believe in the Church as a supernatural society, or in the gospel as revealed truth, can be taken seriously unless it leads to a recognition that the Church's first task is to keep the good news intact. It is better to speak of the habit of mind which this calling requires as "conservationist" rather than "conservative", for the latter word can easily suggest an antiquarian addiction to what is old for its own sake and a blanket resistance to new thinking, and this is not what we are talking about at all. Antiquarianism and obscurantism are vices of the Christian mind, but conservationism is among its virtues.

THE FLIGHT FROM CONFESSING

The Christian conservationist will not refuse to welcome the transcending of ancient conflicts through more attentive listening to each other and deeper theological probing by the divided parties. He will welcome, for instance, the discovery that when the sixteenth-century disputes between Catholics and Protestants over justification and grace, which at the time and for long after seemed incapable of resolution, are reviewed in the light of the deeper problem of the relation between the sovereign Creator and his finite and fallen human children, it is possible to close the gap to such an extent that a Roman divine of the eminence of Hans Küng can conclude that on this subject there is no ultimate contradiction between Karl Barth's teaching and that of the Council of Trent, and profess that "I am unable to see a reason why, as a Catholic theologian, I should not as a whole and with only a few further precisions concur in" the content of Articles 10, 11, 12, and 13, of the Thirty-nine.[1] Or again, the Christian conservationist will welcome the way in which deeper reflection on the nature of priesthood, sacrifice, and the Church has in our day narrowed, if not closed, the gap between Catholics and Protestants on the nature of the Eucharist (see our own Appendix on this). Nor will the conservationist oppose the raising and exploring of new theological questions, evoked by new times, or the attempt to restate old truths in new forms, so as to make them more meaningful for a new age. But he will always ask of every new formulation: "Does it embody the essentials? *Has anything vital been left out?*" And he will oppose heart and soul the habit of mind which may be called *doctrinal minimalism* wherever in the Church he finds it.

What is doctrinal minimalism? It is a habit of mind which in situations of doctrinal tension and questioning seeks and settles for the minimum that will disarm the contenders, and which calculates this minimum in each case by reference to the known views of the parties rather than the revealed truth of Scripture and the apostolic deposit. It is a pragmatic habit of mind, for which questions of truth are evidently of less importance than questions of institutional prosperity. Its concern is not to clarify God's truth on any issue, but to enlarge the area in which men of diverse views may be persuaded to agree to differ so that together they may get on with something else. The minimalist spirit among Anglicans appeared in the humanist circle around Colet in the early sixteenth century, the Cambridge Platonists in the mid-seventeenth, the Latitudinarians of the late seventeenth and eighteenth, Broad Churchmen of the *Essays and Reviews* type in the mid-nineteenth, and many Liberals in the twentieth; and the modern concern for church reunion has given it a new lease of life. To ask, when some new public manifestation of Christian unity is proposed, "What is the minimum of agreement in belief that is necessary for this purpose?"—organic union, full or partial intercommunion, or whatever it may be—is natural, tempting, and perhaps inevitable. *But it is the wrong question, all the same.* It betrays a minimalist approach to doctrine which is poles apart from the attitude from which the creeds took their rise. The new Christian in the Church's early days was not concerned to bargain for the minimum terms on which he could identify himself with the Christian fellowship; his concern, rather,

[1] *Justification*, pp. ix f; cf. p. 44 ff above.

was to proclaim his acceptance of the revelation made by God in Jesus Christ in all its fullness and with all its implications. Equally, the Church's teachers in those days had no interest in devising agreements to differ, on a minimal basis of common belief, with those in whose views they saw the pattern of half- and quarter-truths, with accompanying negations, for which "heresy" is the classical name. Rather, their sense of the organic unity of God's truth led them to see weakness at one point as threatening all, and to regard the removal of this cancer from the body of Christ as the prime task. And any lesser concern, now as then, really calls in question the seriousness of one's belief that revelation took place in any unique and final sense in Jesus Christ at all; for if it did, and if this is God's last word to man, then no duty can be more pressing in any age than to keep knowledge of this revelation in its wholeness from being whittled away and lost.

But this attitude does not seem to appear in the 1968 report of the Anglican–Methodist Commission, any more than it did in the 1963 report of its predecessor. It is true that the Commission was not planning directly for union between the two bodies, only for full communion on a basis of continued independence for the present, and therefore the Commission's brief did not call for the production of a basis of doctrine for a united Church. It is also true that the Commission's reply to the question "What will be the Basis of Faith in the united Church?" was to the effect that "the united Church should publicly stand for all that either Church stood for in separation".[1] Furthermore, an early chapter entitled "Agreement in Doctrine", which enumerates a number of correspondences at the level of official statements on both sides, declares that "the doctrine of our two Churches has been one major subject of discussion throughout" (para. 32). However, the reader is left uneasy. The impression constantly given is that questions of Christian doctrine were considered as tiresome preliminaries, obstacles to be overcome as a means to the more important end of institutional adjustment, rather than as issues which were vital precisely because the preserving of the good news in the Church, and the publishing of it by the Church to the world, was itself the desired outcome of the whole project.

To be sure, the report makes reference to "a wide area of

---

[1] *Anglican–Methodist Unity: The Scheme*, para. 277.

doctrinal agreement already established", to which earlier statements had borne witness (para. 36). The only explicit quotations from, or references to, earlier statements come from the report *Church Relations in England* of 1950 and the *Interim Statement* of 1958, both of which make confident assertions about agreement on fundamental doctrines but omit to expound it in detail. It is, indeed, extraordinary how limited in theological concern, and perfunctory in treating theological issues, the literary products of the Church of England's endeavours towards union since the last war have appeared to be.

What the 1967 *Interim Statement* and the 1968 report offer, instead of the organic exposition of overall theological concord that might have been hoped for, is a trio of lengthy discussions of three particularly obstinate questions, "Scripture and Tradition", "Priesthood and Ministry", and "The Doctrine of Holy Communion: Sacrificial Aspects". It may seem unreasonable to complain that attention was devoted to questions on which *prima facie* disagreement appeared rather than to those on which agreement could be presumed, especially when it was part of the second Commission's stated task to clear up, if it could, the difficulties which the 1963 statements on these three issues had created in many minds. Yet it is not unreasonable to suggest that it was precisely the presumed agreements which needed deeper consideration, and that without this discussion of the other issues could not be satisfactorily carried through. For it is undeniable that the three discussions assume as their starting-point the outlook of sixteenth-century Protestantism as interpreted in the "classical Anglican divines" and the Wesleys (para. 52), and never question this frame of reference, which makes them peculiarly impervious to the kind of rethinking that is going on in the ecumenical realm today. And it is also undeniable that at certain points an uncritical attitude to verbal agreements leads to what can only be described as double-think or at least double-talk. Thus, certain quotations from the 1963 report are held to have "the effect of establishing Holy Scripture as the sole and authoritative source of 'all doctrine required of necessity to eternal salvation', and as the norm and standard of doctrinal and ethical teaching, of worship, and of practice for the Church in every age" (para. 51). However, a little later we read that there are some in both Churches, whose exclusion is unthinkable (though care is taken not to voice approval of their view of the Bible, or any other view of it for that matter), who take the position that both Testaments contain so many "possibilities of error" that "the Church cannot legitimately require belief in more than a limited number of facts [we are not told which] held to be basic to God's revelation" (paras. 59, 63). One could be forgiven for thinking that the affirmation of the sole final authority of Scripture was put in merely to reassure those who might otherwise fear that traditional anti-Roman attitudes were in danger, and that, once the verbal point had been made, the way was deliberately left clear for anyone to treat Scripture as he pleases. Here the cloven hoof of doctrinal minimalism seems to appear, if not indeed of doctrinal indifferentism, which is worse. In any case, what reassurance can statements about the *formal* authority of Scripture give when the question of interpretation—that is, the question how one determines the authoritative *content* of Scripture—is left so completely open? What heresy has there ever been that was not based on erratic and selective private interpretation of the Bible? But the doctrinal minimalist, who seeks agreed formulas on a pragmatic basis and who, once he has found one (in this case, the sole final authority of the Bible), is not prepared to go behind it and see how substantial, or unsubstantial, the agreement really is, will sweep aside such questionings as captious, perverse, and contrary to the true ecumenical spirit.

A RETURN TO CONFESSING

This, however, cannot be admitted. The reunion of the Church is a matter affecting the Christian community as a whole, and needs to be approached in the setting of the Church's contemporary life as a whole. Professed agreements that turn out to be verbal only, and proposals to agree to differ that have only pragmatic and not theological justification, are disruptive, not unitive, in their effect. Already it has become evident that the Anglican–Methodist negotiations have led to strained relations between Methodists on the one hand and Presbyterians and Congregationalists on the other, and between Anglicans on the one hand and Roman Catholics and Orthodox on the other, to say nothing of the tensions created within the Anglican and Methodist Churches themselves. The truth that must be faced here is that any bilateral discussions, whether between Anglicans and Methodists or any other ecclesiastical pairings, are likely to have this effect, since in them the temptation to doctrinal minimalism will be strongest, for reasons which are obvious.

One clear conclusion of our argument is that only as genuinely multilateral discussions towards union come into being is there hope of realizing adequately that oneness in truth which is the necessary basis for any institutional *rapprochement*. For questions of theology, so far from being tedious obstacles to be circumvented if possible and dissolved into indifference or ambiguity if not, are the precise points on which dialogue should be concentrated; and if the dialogue is to be fruitful, all seriously held theologies must take part; and only by such dialogue can a unity of heart and mind in confessing the faith be reached which will enrich the Churches involved in it and further their mission of making known to the modern world the word which God has spoken in Jesus Christ once and for all.

A second conclusion, equally clear, is that a contemporary declaration of faith for a united Church needs to be drawn up as a basis for uniting to form it, and that the abiding status of the declaration within the new body must be agreed from the start. Union schemes today are often content to say simply that a united Church will be free to make its own decisions on current doctrinal issues once it has come into being. This is obviously right and proper within limits, but the limits must be specified. Those who will unite to form the new Church have a right to be assured that "the faith once for all delivered to the saints", the doctrinal heritage which their own Church (as they understand it) has preserved hitherto, will not be put at risk in the merged community. Nor is assurance on this point given sufficiently by the announcing of a general commitment to the historic creeds, or to later documents such as the Thirty-nine Articles for that matter; for though these statements undoubtedly embody the substance of the faith, they were not drawn up in face of modern aberrations, and a professed acceptance of them remains enigmatic till one shows one's hand in relation to the minimizing forms of belief, and doctrinal minimalism as a habit of mind, which are matters of such common occurrence today. (After all, the late Bishop Pike, who sat very loose to some crucial Christian facts, did not hesitate to profess acceptance of the Creed for the purposes of singing!) So a contemporary confession, orientated to current forms of misbelief, must be drawn up, and written into the constitution of the proposed united Church. The importance of the latter point is illustrated by the present union negotiations in New Zealand: here, a contemporary statement of "The Faith we Affirm Together" has been drawn up "for the purposes of union",[1] but not for the united Church, which will be bound in a formal, verbal way to the Lambeth Quadrilateral, but not in a specific way to anything. It is small wonder that a number of Anglicans, contemplating the extreme doctrinal radicalism of the leadership in another of the uniting bodies, should be troubled at the lack of safeguards and the irresponsibility that acceptance of such doctrinal looseness would involve, and should desiderate Declaratory Articles on doctrine, which should reassert crucial Christian truths in direct counter to modern deviations, and which should have permanent constitutional status in the new fellowship. Whether a new Church will have tight or loose doctrinal discipline for its clergy and members is, of course, a distinct question from the doctrinal commitment it will accept (except where the former is so loose as to make any professed doctrinal commitment incredible); and it is the doctrinal commitment that we are talking about at the moment. It must be possible to know in advance that as a corporate body a united Church will stand for the historic faith in its fullness, and only a contemporary confessional statement, given constitutional status in advance, will make this possible.

[1] *Plan for Union* (Joint Commission on Church Union in New Zealand) (1969), sec. 17.

7

The Integration of Ministries

THE OBSTINACY OF THE PROBLEM

We have tackled the question of reunion in England since April 1969 with the sense of being haunted by a ghost. Whatever theology or practice commanded our agreement, it has been confidently foretold that we should come to grief on this question. To pretend the ghost was not there would solve nothing, whilst to attempt to exorcize it (we were told) would merely drive it to haunt us more persistently. For ourselves we have tried to remain confident in God that if he could bring us to one mind on contextual questions, so he would dispatch the ghost for us also. And so it has proved. In dealing with other questions, more fundamental in themselves, we have found ourselves driven to one clear mind on this question. In refusing to make a solution to this question top priority on our agenda, we have come to it in its proper place and found it not unyielding. But we must emphasize at the outset that our solution is only set forward in the context of the whole book, and particularly of the chapters preceding this one, and without them we should have to delete this chapter also. The integration of ministries is not, we dare affirm, capable of satisfactory piecemeal solution. And it seems passing strange that the late Scheme attempted to solve this question first whilst delaying most of the others—and that the two Churches in 1965 voted through their decision-making bodies that the integration of ministries had been satisfactorily solved[1] (contrary to the actual voting in their two denominations), whilst everything else was either still in the melting-pot, or could in principle still be returned thither. If, therefore, anyone has turned from the list of contents to read this chapter first of all, we respectfully ask him to think again and read the book in its logical order. This question does not yield to slick "Open Sesames", and none are provided here.

[1] The principle of the Service of Reconciliation was accepted in the adoption by both bodies of "the broad outline" of the 1963 Scheme. The daunting *local* returns in both Churches are summarized in the Introduction, p. 12.

We suspect that the size of the problem has been exaggerated by the emotional atmosphere of the confrontation. The fact that the divide between rigid episcopalian and rigid anti-episcopalian may have become narrow at most other points has only served to focus and deepen the cleavage here. The fewer other points of dissension there have been, the more trouble has concentrated around this one unsolved question. Solutions have therefore been approached by negotiating from sharply separated premises, and we think that this dual standpoint has affected the outcome. For ourselves, although some differences of emphasis remain, we have found our premisses so close to each other (after doing all the earlier work of this book) that we have felt the process of building here to be different in principle from that which we detect in other schemes.

The Service of Reconciliation is the classic expression of this "dual premisses" procedure. We have felt it necessary to expose its fallacies at length,[1] not because there is anything particularly new to say on the point, but simply because there is little evidence that the points we made separately in the past have been treated seriously. We content ourselves here with pointing out that the Service purports to hold together under one umbrella mutually exclusive positions. It would be better (because more honest) to despair of a solution altogether than to build one in this way. The mere fact that one cannot see a way through a maze is no excuse for running up a cul-de-sac which everyone can see is *not* a way through.

The other major existing solution is the one which was followed in South India. This frankly attracts us more than the Service of Reconciliation. It has an honesty and an openness which the Service of Reconciliation palpably lacks. The South India Christians went into their union with their eyes open, whereas we in England have been confronted by a scheme which required of us that we should shut our eyes at the point of entry. However, we realize that South India has many residual problems, and we do know that the operation of the "Pledge" has been felt by a tiny few as an unfair rendering of them into second-class ministers.[2] In addition, there has been one area, Nandyal, where Anglicans have been unable for reasons of conscience to enter the

[1] See Appendix 5, pp. 193–201 below.
[2] This was set out by Marcus Ward in "'The Church of South India and the Anglican–Methodist Report': A Personal Note" (TAMU Leaflet no. 2, 1964).

union, and there have been highly disruptive shock-waves around the whole Anglican Communion springing from the integration of ministries in South India. None of these things would of themselves change our direction, but we view them as warnings that we cannot simply adopt a "South India" pure and simple as the way through our troubles in England. If South India has lessons to teach the ecumenical world, as we believe it has, yet the twenty and more years since its inauguration have also lessons to teach. We have thus not found a ready-made solution to hand, and were thus not able to offer an easy way out when we felt obliged to oppose the late Scheme in May and July 1969.[1]

AN APPROACH TO AN ANSWER

Our earlier chapters have set out certain principles which demarcate the ground within which a solution has to be found. Each of these is the product of the argument in its respective chapter, and each must therefore be referred back to its chapter for substantiation. Here the principles are merely invoked.

The first element in the answer is that the integration will result in an episcopally ordered ministry.[2] The historic episcopate will be integrated with the life of a united Church including Anglicans from the start. There would be no objection to consecrating for the office of bishop men whose existing ministry had been conferred by Presbyterian-type ordination. All ordinations within a united Church would be performed by bishops from the start. Here is ground agreed by all Anglican Churches in negotiation with non-episcopal Churches, and largely accepted by the latter.

Secondly, ordination to any of the three recognized official orders of the ministry is once for life to each order.[3] This means that no integration of ministries can be based upon a sheer admission that particular ministers *both* are ordained *and* need to be ordained again. We must seek some form of integration which does justice to the truth of the calling of men (even in divided Churches) to be ministers for life in the Church of God on earth, and nothing less. This in turn means that no other ceremony which purports not to be an ordination, but in practical terms

---

[1] See the relevant parts of Appendixes 1 and 2 on pp. 165 and 174–5 below.
[2] This is argued in ch. 4, pp. 72–83 above.
[3] See ch. 4, pp. 83–4 above.

supersedes ordination as the basic qualification for ministry, can be considered either.[1]

Thirdly, a united Church is not to have two or more classes of ministers within it—or, if on some analysis it has, the effects of this must be reduced to barest minimum. It might indeed be tolerable that other Churches should view the united Church as having two classes of ministers, if the united Church itself had full mutual internal recognition and acceptance of its own ministers. It would certainly be more tolerable than having internal divisions. But the ideal should remain of only one class of ministers, such that if any two or more classes were involved at inauguration, they would be assimilated into one, preferably at the outset but at worst *in via*.

Fourthly, the ministry is not at any time to lose its structural relationship with the Church. Stage One of the late Scheme detached the unification of ministries from the unification of the Churches within which they existed, and in theological terms ended with a well-dressed non-event. We cannot contemplate uniting ministries as a separate venture from uniting Churches, and we thus find our minds hardening more and more in favour of a one-stage scheme. Just as the ministry is not logically prior to the Church,[2] so to unite ministries as a detached venture out of any relationship to the union of Churches is to argue in practical terms the most abhorrently "pipeline" theology—that the Church is simply a function of the ministry, and the union of the former a function of the union of the latter. The setting of the ministry within the Church argues that union of one must accompany union of the other, and accompany it not only by chronological co-incidence but also by organic interrelationship.

SOME SOLUTIONS EXPLORED

In the light of the above principles we may examine certain proposed forms of integration to see if they square with the theology we conceive fundamental to a scheme. These can be simply set out as follows.

(a) *Episcopal Ordination ab initio of Non-Episcopal Ministers.* This would of course lead to the outcome of a single ministry with undoubted orders. We are unable to recommend it, however,

---

[1] See Appendix 5, p. 204 below.   [2] See ch. 4, p. 71 above.

and that not simply on the grounds that the relevant ministers would probably not accept it. We ourselves cannot regard men already ordained within their denominations as simply laymen, and, as stated above, a second ordination would violate one of the principles we are most concerned to safeguard.[1]

(b) *Mutual Ordination ab initio.* This is a totally spurious solution. Because some Anglicans have doubted the sufficiency or propriety or acceptability of non-episcopal orders, the situation is levelled out by a perverse theological socialism, everybody expressing equal doubts about his own orders and everybody else's. Spoof mutuality for the sake of charity (or, less happily, as a snare) is dealt with elsewhere.[2] Here it merely remains to add that the whole concept of mutuality depends upon a bilateral situation of confrontation, and we both reject this presupposition and point out that continuity with the past and ordination once for life are both jettisoned by this method.

(c) *Conditional Episcopal Ordination of Non-Episcopal Ministers.* This has some advantages which ordination *ab initio* lacks. It defends the concept of ordination once-for-life, whilst enabling the recipients to defend their previous ministry. It squarely deals with the actual problem which has existed, and does so without dragging those already episcopally ordained into the toils of further problems about their own orders. If this proposal had been the basis for Stage One of the late Scheme, Anglicans would have had little ground for opposing it if Methodists had been prepared to accept it. We are, however, assured that Methodists never would have accepted it, and we take that seriously.

In any case, although the answer is the right shape, it is of curiously artificial materials. For the problem has first to be restated as "Have these men been ordained or not?" instead of the more obvious "What sort of ordination have these men got?". This is comparable to curing the common cold by first giving the patient bronchitis (on the grounds that this is easier to cure). The answer works, but at a cost of some professional unscrupulousness. If the patient would like it that way (and after all he is being

---

[1] The existing Anglican practice of ordaining *ab initio* non-episcopal ministers who seek to minister in the Church of England presents some grave difficulties. What we propose in terms of union is, however, a strictly separate question, and the Church of England's domestic practice is irrelevant to it.
[2] See Appendix 5, p. 203 below.

guaranteed a cure), who shall say him nay? But, if he would not, then no doctor must be allowed to force it on him.[1]

(d) *Mutual Conditional Ordination.* This has most of the disadvantages of mutual ordination *ab initio* listed out above—except of course that theoretically it does not involve an abandonment of the once-for-life concept. In fact, a ceremony of this sort would in practical terms go far towards being a totally new rite, superseding all previous ordinations, and by that token only a hand's breadth away from the recent Service of Reconciliation.

(e) *Mutual Acceptance with a Pledge.* This is the South India method. We have stated our sympathy with it above. However, the Pledge worries us. There can be two ways of looking at it. One is simply to say that uniting is a dynamic event, which remains a continuous experience in the life of the united Church. It is thus over-scrupulous, unwise, and probably self-defeating, to insist on solving every problem at the outset. The Pledge enables the Churches to join, with an interim solution to the problem of the ministerial integration, but without driving out those who are hesitant to accept it.[2] It postpones certain problems rather than the whole experience of reunion, and simultaneously claims that the context of living in a united Church is the best framework for ultimately reaching a solution.

There is another way of looking at South India. It is possible to say that the Pledge is simply a device to enable the parties to a contract to opt out of the implications of that to which they have put their hands. On this basis it is less than honest to add the "escape clause" to the contract. The fact that few in South India have taken advantage of the Pledge is neither here nor there— the point is that the inclusion of the provision in the contract is (on this analysis) the very reverse of the symbol of love and trust it has usually been dressed up to be. This objection to the Pledge may be an overstatement (for Catholics who took part in the union at all had to belong to a Church which officially recognized non-episcopal ministers and at this level they simply could not opt out of the implications of the contract), but we have felt its force.

---

[1] There may be a case for conditional ordination in a less prominent or significant role, and we return to this on pp. 219-20 below.

[2] This was of course equally true in South India of the reverse side of the "Pledge"—that no set liturgy would be forced on any congregation not desiring it.

The effect of this on a "South India" in England is discussed by S. Barrington-Ward in a recent article. He writes:

One must also be allowed a certain degree of scepticism about the sudden new fashionableness of South India in certain quarters. Some of the most surprising people, previously disdainful of this method, now let little hints drop that after all they begin to feel that it could meet all their requirements. What is it that has come to attract them so? Could it be that there is a certain, albeit unconscious, unreality in this new preference? Perhaps it is the conscience clause in the South India scheme which most appeals, with the assurance it conveys that no minister or congregation would ever find themselves forced together against their convictions with those whom they still could not inwardly recognize. It would then become, unbeknown, almost the central feature of the scheme for its new admirers; a last device, one might fear, for dodging the inevitable unity, rather than a genuine way of achieving it.[1]

This is a distressing piece of writing, by one who says that his original intention would have been, if the 1968 Scheme failed, to "return to first principles and formulate from scratch a South India scheme".[2] But if he had been a *Catholic* pleading that morally Catholics had little right to support a South India type of integration with mental reservations of this sort, then his thrust would have carried some weight. We have felt this objection, and are agreed that no "South India" *simpliciter* will meet the case. The difficulties of the Pledge in relation to England have been vastly overstated (as a backdoor and crafty furtherance of the late

---

[1] "Is the Union Scheme dead?", *Theology* (October 1969), pp. 434-40. The extract quoted is from p. 437.

[2] Barrington-Ward is justifying his failure to revert to a South India scheme by the fact that apparently some Catholics might now like that approach. If they are in favour, then he is opposed (whereas previously he had been opposed to South India simply because Catholics were *not* in favour). He does not, of course, know why Catholics should now favour South India, and he feels bound to put the most sinister possible motive upon their advocacy. He also seems in favour of merging ministers and congregations contrary to their consciences, a point which would certainly apply as much under the late Scheme as under a South India scheme without a Pledge. And he proceeds to an argument about the late scheme which would change no one's mind, but is apparently thought to make the Scheme viable. The message seems to be: "If you knock away our arguments for the Scheme we'll go on finding new ones, *ad nauseam*."

Scheme), but, lest we should appear to fall under any of the strictures set out above, we renounce any interest in anything comparable to the Pledge. We see a way in which the good side of the Pledge—that is, the fostering of a *growing* unity within which previously intractable problems prove easier of solution—can be implemented in England without recourse to this South India means.

THE BEST WAY FORWARD

These then are not viable possibilities and we have not occupied ourselves with them. Rather, the principles we have invoked have led us to one clear solution—the "adoption" of existing ministries into the presbyterate of an episcopally structured ministry, without a further ordination or quasi-ordination *and without a Pledge*. We write this maintaining our previous insistence that our whole position stands or falls together. It is therefore important that the clear episcopal structuring of the Church and agreement on the nature of the ministry in relation to the sacraments should be seen as the context within which such acceptance should and could occur. Granted that the context promises to maintain those theological principles we have already set out, we believe that existing ministers of the denominations with which the Church of England would be likely to be able to reach agreement could be accepted as presbyters within the total ministry of the new united episcopal Church. Ministers in these denominations would be "adopted" into such a structure, but only in such a way that the organic relation of the presbyterate to the episcopate is not called permanently in question. We see no other way to do justice to convictions that they are not laymen to be received as candidates for ordination, they are not to be ordained twice, they are not to be given some ceremony superseding ordination, and they are to be taken seriously in their own claims to be ordained in the sight of God. Yet the context is vital, as we must also give expression to our own judgement that through its disciplinary norms the united Church should preserve the invariable practice of episcopal ordination within itself, and should extend itself down time and through space by an episcopally ordered structure.

At the same time we are serious in renouncing a Pledge. We could each of us minister with good conscience in such a united Church, and could anticipate in such a context having no scruples as to the "pedigree" of the ministers from whom we ever received Communion. We would not want to advocate such a form of union, if we were not ourselves ready in principle to follow out the logic of our advocacy.

Nevertheless, to come to such a conclusion ourselves—and it has been no easy path for us all—is not to say that we would lightly thrust others into the same situation. To quote from the Barrington-Ward article again, we would certainly feel that there *must* be "assurance...that no minister or congregation would ever find themselves forced together against their convictions with those whom they still could not inwardly recognize". This is simply to declare ourselves Christian! And we would anticipate that in the absence of a Pledge this assurance must be given by the simple expedient of inaugurating a united Church in a piecemeal way territorially, leaving the existing denominations to exist alongside each other in every place where conscience, even untutored conscience, might so decree. In the next chapters we set out the procedure we should expect (which is actually demanded much more by our ideal of local organic union than by this method of integrating ministries), and it will be clear that on this basis no Pledge is necessary. Only those already prepared for every feature of the basis of union will be entering the united Church, and they will need no safeguards against each other.

To put this in other words, our willingness for far greater pluriformity in practice, if it be related to clear doctrinal norms, has its proper outworking in a union scheme in which ministers with orders of different pedigree take their place alongside each other, whilst the Church in which they serve takes *its* place alongside the other Churches in England. But in each case—ministers within Church, and Church within Churches—although different ways exist, the trends are properly and irreversibly set for the future, and there is built into the present a clear statement of what that future will be, both doctrinally and practically. This we conceive to be a logical outworking of the dynamic principle of union, of life through death, and it is one within which we see all our original principles, to be safeguarded in the integration of ministries, as fully implemented.

Two further features of the outworking need some discussion, and tentative answers will help to etch more boldly the theological priorities we observe in setting up this pattern.

(a) *Relations with Ministries in other Churches.* Obviously we would wish that the ministry of a united Church should be fully interchangeable with the parent ministries of the parent Churches. But we have already made it clear above that we give this a lower priority than the securing to the united ministry of an internal unity. We thus make the following points. We would not urge a change in the Church of England's rules, unless or until this arises through the Lambeth recommendation that full communion with South India should be considered.[1] This would mean that, although all ministers of the Church of England would in principle be eligible to minister in the united Church, the reverse would not be true. The non-episcopal Churches in turn would probably give full recognition to the united Church's ministry, but there might come a time when some restrictions were placed by the united Church upon the recognition of non-episcopal ministers. This would not necessarily be by a single once-for-all decision of the united Church, but might well arise as individual dioceses took more or less permanent form. Even then, there would be no inevitable barrier put up against non-episcopal ministers, but we would suggest that the rules governing their recognition should come up for review every five years at diocesan level. Thus again the pluriform situation would be maintained. Nor would a review necessarily result in a yes-or-no answer—there might arise a situation in which a diocese ruled that some of its parishes were still in transition, but others should now be served invariably by episcopally ordained presbyters. We provide for a review purely to give canonical shape to our conviction that a transitional period is requisite, without either taking the interim for granted as a permanent solution or foreclosing the interim period by an arbitrary advance decision.[2]

(b) *Conditional Ordination.* Although we have said above[3] that we cannot contemplate a mandatory imposition of conditional ordination on those who do not want it, we also refused to rule it out altogether. We cannot view this as a necessary element in the inauguration of organic union, and would discountenance any attempts to make it so. Nevertheless, we can see a situation in

---

[1] *The Lambeth Conference 1968: Resolutions and Reports,* Resolution 48(b), p. 43. Cf. *Intercommunion Today,* p. 124, paras. 218–20.
[2] The sort of timescale we would envisage is discussed on pp. 138 and 153 below.
[3] See pp. 114–5 above.

which there might be a place for it. There appear to exist some non-episcopal ministers who have doubts about the status of their ministry. It is not for us to judge whether these doubts spring from theological or non-theological factors, but we do feel the necessity of meeting the case. It is a case which might prove all the more virulent in a united Church containing ministers with different pedigrees. What can a minister so afflicted do? At the moment he can seek to enter the ministry of the Church of England by episcopal ordination. This, however, would hardly be open to him in the united Church which would stand by the principle of ordination once-for-life. We think that he might be allowed to seek conditional ordination by a bishop in the united Church, but this should be permitted only after he had first served a stated number of years within the Church. Such a provision could be made only for the sake of the individual's own conscience, and could not be, and should not appear to be, a requirement of the Church itself.[1]

Granted these provisions, held together as a single approach to the problem, we believe that every existing minister's conscience can be respected both at entry into union and in the continuing life of a united Church, whilst we also envisage that the situation will allow men to free themselves from confrontation complexes and change their minds on these issues. Those who long for union on such terms would be able to be involved; those who do not would be able to wait and continue their ministry in their existing Church or denomination.

[1] There could conceivably be another situation in which a conditional ordination might arise. A non-episcopal minister with full confidence in his own orders might find himself in an area where a number of communicants insisted on trekking off to some Anglican church a distance away for Communion. If he had reason to think that this was because of his orders (as opposed to his personal gifts, etc.), then he might be allowed to seek a conditional ordination *purely for their sake*. This is always possible even for a man defending his own orders. It does not imply necessary doubt on his own part. We would think it unfortunate to shut up such a man to a situation which otherwise he could not alleviate. But we think the provision would be rarely, if ever, invoked.

NOTE

THE FORM AND MANNER OF INTEGRATION

We realize that the general principles set out above may not sufficiently indicate the procedure we have in mind, and we have therefore felt it good to make some detailed proposals. The detail is simply one expression of the principles, and there might well be others. We have sought a procedure which is neither an ordination nor a quasi-ordination on the one hand nor a simple licensing on the other. We have devised it to include both episcopally ordained ministers and others, and *mutatis mutandis* it could also be used if an Anglican bishop were to be received into a united Church to be a bishop in it.

The Ordinal would be the basic place where the doctrine and functions of the ministry were set out, and it could well be that the existing Anglican–Methodist Ordinal would offer a good starting-point in compiling the requisite texts. A united Church would need to have a single Ordinal, and its Ordinal would need to be one of its doctrinal formulas. The Preface to the Ordinal might well run as follows:

PREFACE TO THE ORDINAL

[The first paragraph would describe the continuity of the Church of God from the Apostles' time, and would lead to an assertion that there exist in the Church particular ministries for the shepherding of the flock and the building up of the whole body.[1]]

The uniting Churches [stated if necessary] have sought to practise a continuity of such ministries by setting men apart with the authority of the Church for the ministry of Word and Sacrament. The united Church continues the orders of bishop, presbyter, and deacon as the Church of England previously received and continued them, and the respective functions of these three orders are sufficiently, though not exhaustively, set out in the services for ordaining ministers which follow.

Although the united Church receives the threefold orders that they "may be continued, and reverently used and esteemed" (as

[1] Compare the Preface to the proposed Anglican–Methodist Ordinal.

was declared in the Preface to the 1550 and subsequent Anglican Ordinals), although it rules that none shall be ordained within its ministry save by a bishop and by the forms attached hereto, yet it receives also as presbyters in the Church of God those ministers of all the uniting Churches who make the requisite declaration in the presence of the bishop of their diocese, and are received by him with the requisite form.

THE REQUISITE DECLARATION
BY MINISTERS OF THE UNITING CHURCHES

I, A. B., having been ordained to the $\begin{cases} \text{ministry within the Church} \\ \text{priesthood within the Church} \end{cases}$
of God according to the rites of the [e.g. Methodist] Church, $\Big\}$ do
of God according to the rites of the Church of England,[1]
now apply to you, bishop of —— in the united Church, for recognition and acceptance as a presbyter in the Church of God in the presbyterate of the united Church. I solemnly attest my acceptance of the confession of faith and constitution of this Church, and in particular of the threefold structure of the ministry, and I promise that canonical obedience which is due from a presbyter to his bishop according to the constitution of this Church.

THE RECEPTION BY THE BISHOP

The Bishop shall stretch out his hands towards him and say:

I, A.B., bishop of —— in the united Church, do recognize and accept you as a presbyter in the Church of God, now to serve within the presbyterate of this diocese in the threefold ministry of this Church. I now commit to you authority to exercise your ministry within this Church wherever you may be called and licensed. May God use your ministry to his great glory. [A blessing might then follow.]

---

[1] Those who had been ordained to the priesthood within the Church of Rome, or indeed within other Churches of the Anglican Communion, would supply the appropriate description here.

PART THREE

The Growth of the Building

"The whole structure...grows into a holy temple in the Lord."
Ephesians 2. 21

This third part of the book goes on to an outline scheme. This is orientated solely towards the situation in England today, and is not intended to be immediately applicable elsewhere. The scheme proceeds by invoking the theological and practical principles set up in the first two parts, and working from them to sharp-edged proposals for actual union today.

8

A One-Stage Scheme

We have now reached the place where sufficient ground has been tested and marked out, sufficient foundations have been laid, and we can start to build. In so doing we would refer back to our own statement in the Introduction[1] that the same ground, and even the same foundations, might admit of other buildings. We do not know. We merely affirm that we have found the outline scheme which we go on to build in the next seven brief chapters a satisfying out-working of the principles so far established. We make no claim that this is the only possible construction.

Our starting-point is that a scheme should be one-stage. This conviction has admittedly matured as we have pondered the more on the late Scheme, with its curious two-stage approach. We have called this "a freak of history",[2] and as such it must take its place in history. It is a freak—partly because it springs from the freakish suggestion of Lord Fisher that the Free Churches should try out episcopacy on their own ground, partly because a Stage Two was later added to his suggestion when it was too late to question Stage One. The freak has been so long with us that we tend to forget how odd it is. We even have to argue against it, when the proper procedure would really be to assume that a one-stage scheme had the *prima facie* claims, and our task was simply to lay the onus of proof on Lord Fisher and his successors. However, as they have succeeded in getting the freak on to the table, we accept that they have *prima facie* claims and the onus is now on us. Our thinking the matter through has led us to a surer mind than a mere accepting of *prima facie* claims could ever have done, and to that extent we feel, not for the first time, the beneficiaries from other people's mistakes.

---

[1] See pp. 20–4 above.
[2] Reprinted on p. 116 in Appendix 1, where the whole quotation would serve well to introduce the theme of this chapter.

DIFFICULTIES IN A TWO-STAGE SCHEME

These fall into two categories: those associated with Stage One and those associated with Stage Two.

1. *Difficulties at Stage One.* There are five of these which spring to mind.

(a) Quite apart from the internal problems of the Service of Reconciliation,[1] the whole concept of integrating ministries in advance of uniting Churches is extremely dubious. It suggests a status and existence for ministries independent of their ecclesial context. It teaches that the Church is at best a function of the ministry or at worst has no relation to the problem of reconciliation at all. None of this was eased in its larger significance by the building in of a token place for the laity to greet each other at the Service of Reconciliation.

(b) The very recognition of the Methodist Church given at Stage One was self-defeating for the organic local unity that ought to have been kept in view. The Church of England, which has a practice built round the *principle* of parishes (though not always well exhibited in its inherited forms), stands for the idea of one church in each place,[2] and seeks to manifest this as best it can. To have brought the Methodists into sacramental relations with their local Anglicans whilst they retained their distinct life would have been to throw away the "one church in each place" pattern, without any guarantee of local unity to restore it. This ran dangerously near to ecclesiastical indifferentism.

(c) Furthermore, the parallel episcopate envisaged would have done the same thing at diocesan level as the failure to unite congregations did at the local level. If episcopacy is commended as a focus of unity,[3] then parallel episcopates make nonsense of the commendation.

(d) A further problem arose in connection with the shape of episcopacy as proposed in Methodism. The bishops concerned were apparently to have had no pastoral or governmental powers adhering to them by virtue of their office.[4] Only one bishop a year

---

[1] These are dealt with fully on pp. 193–207 in Appendix 5.
[2] We have argued for this in the context of reunion in ch. 3, pp. 63–4 above.
[3] See pp. 70 and 79 in ch. 4 above.   [4] *Scheme*, paras. 113–39.

(the President of Conference) would have had the power of ordaining, and then, like a drone after its brief flight, would have ceased from his supposedly distinctive function. The proposal read not as making people bishops to give them powers, but as making them bishops as an extra accolade and dignity to reward them well for exercising the powers they already had on other grounds. The two obvious cartoon features of Anglican episcopacy are first the angle of pomp and dignity, and secondly that of the "gimmick for validating orders". These, and these alone, were precisely the features of episcopacy it was proposed to convey to the Methodist Church! Could anything have been more destructive of a healthy understanding of *episkope*?[1]

(*e*) The biggest objection to the two-stage Scheme was that it postponed every tricky problem *except* that of the ministry. If there were really a deep-felt desire for union in the two Churches, then a bold programme for reform could have been put before them. But the existing, often superficial, desire could only be sustained by a promise that major changes would be a long way off. This was open to criticism in several ways. First, in the tidying up of the ministry it offered the process no support in ecclesiology—it was simply and nakedly a "pedigree of orders" question. Secondly, in speaking of union without mutual reform it sold a static and unhelpful concept of the goal. Thirdly, in postponing questions instead of focusing them it incurred the charge of duplicity—for men did not know how far-reaching their votes for unity would be. Stage One had more than a hint of a spider asking a fly into its attractive parlour.

2. *Difficulties at Stage Two.*   These number three.

(*a*) There was no guarantee that Stage Two could ever be achieved. There were even occasional attempts to *defend* the Scheme by saying Stage Two might never occur! Because there was no certainty of agreements in the multitude of spheres in which they were

---

[1] It was ironical, to say the least, to find Hugh Montefiore saying in a letter to *The Times* on 11 July 1969 that, as the Church of England is episcopal and 93 % of the bishops were in favour of the Scheme, the job of everyone else was simply to trust the bishops who had the moral right to take the decision for us. The decision itself was of course to produce in Methodism a class of "bishops" who would have been the servants of Conference—which suggests that Canon Montefiore, on his own view of episcopacy, ought to have been opposing a Scheme so inimical to that view.

needed, it was impossible (morally if not physically) to pledge to each other that there would be agreement. For all we could tell, this pledge might have been comparable to a promise made by mountaineers going up different mountains that they would meet at the top. It threatened to impale us on the horns of a dilemma. Either it would be dishonoured (which would have been a moral failure) or it would be a hammer to make us accept *any* solution of the outstanding problems uncritically.

(*b*) One major problem of Stage Two was not even listed: the problem of local union. The Scheme did not spell out, even with reference to Stage Two, that congregations should unite or might have to. This single point affected deeply the costliness of voting— for whilst many who desired union could take it for granted that this point was included (and would have viewed it all as rather a waste of time without), yet many others could view the Scheme as painless and therefore could vote for it at no personal cost. The sheer vagueness of Stage Two was a great encouragement to cheap voting, and thus no real test of how genuine was the desire of the Churches for the cost of unity. The overall impression left by this studied silence is one of laxity approaching dishonesty.

(*c*) There was at least one point where Stage Two was in formal contradiction to Stage One. Stage One insisted that the laying on of a bishop's hands was vital for an authorized ministry, but Stage Two included a further pledge that all ministers of World Methodism would be acceptable within the united Church. This was like heading south with the stated intention of reaching Scotland. And, although it was not integral to the whole concept of a two-stage scheme, it was the fairly predictable outcome of adding a Stage Two to the differing basic assumptions on which the Conversationalists started work in 1956.

REASONS FOR A ONE-STAGE SCHEME

These can be read off the criticisms above, and may be listed under three heads:

1. *An integrated theology.* Church, and ministry, episcopacy and sacraments—these can all receive treatment as one entity, and distortion of any of them in practice can be minimized.

2. *A programme for reform.* Church government, Church and State, appointments of ministers, finance, overseas links, all these and a host more have to go back into the melting-pot. A one-stage scheme focuses the difficult problems instead of evading them. It calls upon *this* generation to die in order to live, instead of asking this generation to vote that their successors should.

3. *A continuing catalyst.* If it be granted that not all problems can be solved at one fell swoop, yet the continuing *experience* of union should provide a far better context for continuing to work at them than the twin-Church position still obtaining during Stage One of the two-stage Scheme.

The *objections to a one-stage scheme* seem to boil down to two:

1. *Constitutional questions.* These were the starting-point in Lord Fisher's advocacy of keeping the Churches separate. But once the pledge to proceed to Stage Two was involved even a two-stage scheme would have necessitated large-scale constitutional changes. To this extent Stage Two cancelled out Lord Fisher's rationale for Stage One. If we have to come to constitutional questions some day let us do it now. The proposals we have to make will keep this problem down to its absolute minimum.

2. *Practical (or psychological) questions.* If it is impossible to get a whole denomination to accept a two-stage scheme which evades most of the problems, how could any denomination ever be brought to accept a one-stage scheme in which the problems loomed large? We have ourselves repeatedly insisted that moral unanimity is needed for a union scheme,[1] and it might well appear that we are banishing all hopes of progress far beyond the horizon by insisting on a one-stage scheme alongside that criterion of acceptability. Again, we can only say that to read on may disabuse the critic of this notion. But he will see that we *have* held strongly to our "moral unanimity" policy.

We are bound to state that the difficulties are considerable, but not overwhelming—and, lying as they do largely in the fields of law and psychology, they do not persuade us to abandon our theological principles. They merely present a challenge to us to orientate our "one-stage" theology aright.

[1] This is spelled out on p. 171 in our July 1969 statement.

9

Building Bit by Bit

In ch. 7[1] we set out in anticipation of this discussion a brief outline of a one-stage procedure, the nub of the matter being expressed in this way: "[we would recommend] the simple expedient of inaugurating a united Church in a piecemeal way territorially, leaving the existing denominations to exist alongside each other in every place where conscience, even untutored conscience, might so decree". This is the conclusion, novel in the history of English ecumenical discussion, to which we have come. This will do justice to the various principles on which we wish to build far better than any other procedure which has suggested itself to us. And it is a principle which, if novel in England, has some precedent in South India. As South India is the only existing union in which Anglicans have joined, we may well look cautiously in that direction for help.

ONE AREA AT A TIME

It is perhaps worth stopping to ask ourselves why it was a *South* India union. The reasons are not hard to seek. Two of the uniting Churches had a specifically South Indian organization, and it was only in South India that the third, the Anglican, was in a position to proceed at the requisite pace. Furthermore, the definition of "South" was extremely untidy—leaving out originally the North Tamil Church Council of the South India United Church, leaving out to this day the Anglicans in Nandyal, including the northern tip of Ceylon (which was included in one of the Methodist districts), and having no defined limits as to where its borders would ultimately come.[2] This in turn meant that for the Anglicans, although moral unanimity was needed[3] in the four dioceses concerned (and

---

[1] See p. 118 above.

[2] See the amazingly untidy situation revealed by the maps in Sundkler, *The Church of South India* (Lutterworth 1954), pp. 446–7. The only comparable untidiness in the Church of England today is the inclusion in the diocese of Canterbury of the archdeaconry of Croydon.

[3] It was not only needed, it was supplied. Cf. the form of the resolution passed by the General Council of the Church of India, Burma and Ceylon: "That

where it was lacking in Nandyal no one was forced into union), yet it was *not* needed through the whole of the Church of India, Burma, and Ceylon. It was in fact accepted by the General Council of that Anglican province by simple majorities, and in the House of Bishops by a mere 6 votes to 4. It is said that it was only when it was finally brought home to Dr Hubback, the Bishop of Assam, over the lunch-break, that he would *not* be committing his own diocese to going the same route to reunion that he was persuaded to support the motion that the South Indian dioceses should form with others the Church of South India. His deciding vote, based on the concept of pluriformity and doing what you can where you can, swung the day.[1] We have a lesson to learn.

ROOM FOR GROWTH

This is the corollary of the last point. If union schemes start in an untidy way, they must leave scope for further growth. This means not only an open-ended pattern of union, which will encourage negotiations with other denominations (such as C.S.I. is currently pursuing with the various Lutheran bodies in South India[2]), but also an open-sided pattern able to gather in the various sections of the original denominations which did not join in originally. In South India this latter principle has seen three further outworkings. In the first place, one of the South India United Church area councils (the North Tamil Church Council) did not join the union. 1950 saw the accession of this section, the opposition within the council having somewhat faded once the actual experience of union had begun among their neighbours. The second accession was the transferring of twelve parishes from the North Indian diocese of Bombay to the C.S.I. diocese of Mysore in 1963. The third was the coming into the Mysore diocese of the South Kanara and

this Council...finally adopts the Scheme of Church Union in South India... in order to permit [the four dioceses] to carry out *their practically unanimous desire* to enter into union..." The italics are ours. They point up a factor in South India which even some South Indian churchmen have forgotten when urging the late Scheme in England.

[1] Sundkler's account (op. cit., p. 334) is here bodied out by the personal recollections of the clinical theologian Dr Frank Lake, who was a lay missionary in that General Council in January 1945. The clergy vote was 38-10, the laity 31-7.

[2] This question of further expanding union is one of the most telling logical arguments against the Service of Reconciliation pattern; see the discussion on p. 200 in Appendix 5.

Coorg District of the Base Mission Church (Presbyterian) in 1968. Meanwhile the Nandyal area had become a North India diocese (though geographically in the C.S.I. area), and the Jaffna diocese in Ceylon had joined the negotiations for church union in Ceylon—known as the Lanka Scheme. In this flexibility in continuing union we have again a lesson to learn.

AN OUTLINE OF PROCEDURE

If we try to build a one-stage scheme in England according to these principles, there are certain adaptations we shall have to make. The major one concerns the size of areas allowed to opt in or opt out of the union. The multiplication of denominations, even in small villages, is a feature of the English church scene which by contrast was virtually unknown in South India. There the principle of comity meant that different areas "belonged" to different missionary societies, and these in turn practised "one church in each place" as the pattern of church life. Thus the pains and stresses of uniting local congregations were involved in the South India union neither at the point of inauguration nor subsequently. In England we have to contend with severe and deeply entrenched local division.

Because of the principles we have outlined earlier we should be unwilling to allow competing local congregations to join a united Church while retaining their separation from each other. The whole concept of dying to live (quite apart from the results of Methodist union since 1932) suggests that local uniting must accompany entry into the united Church. This in turn indicates that accessions by this means would come only slowly, and that unions in a very small area, perhaps no greater than existing Anglican parishes, would have to be acceptable. The actual areas involved would need to be negotiated in each case, but the difference in concept between an English "bit-by-bit" and a South Indian one emerges at sight.

Thus we would look for a united Church to grow up between the existing denominations by accessions from existing congregations spread slowly over the years. The united Church would start as one or two isolated parish-type areas, grow into an archipelago, and eventually approach a solid shape in region after region, until the participating denominations finally disappeared and a new

English Church had replaced them. In every case the transfer would occur only when the local Christians were agreed in desiring it, and, although the parent denomination and the united Church authorities would be involved in negotiating, the local church or churches would be granted full powers to take the decision for themselves.

The earlier conclusion that the Church of God is an organic unity, to be neither dismembered nor atomized, may at first sight militate against this "congregationalization" of the problem of organic unity. If so, a helpful paradigm may be found in the baptism of individuals. The candidate is moving from one corporate organic whole (the body of Adam, in Pauline terms) to another corporate organic whole (the body of Christ). The fact that the individual must individually take that decision in no sense militates against the organic character of the Church of God. If the transfer be "voluntarist", yet the resultant state is organic. If the Church summons the individual to baptism, yet in receiving him it incorporates him into the whole. By definition the transfer *must* be individual, but that has no implications for the corporate character of either the old body or the new.

Mutatis mutandis, this should help to explain the process we here advocate. Obviously, we make no such strong division between the old and the new as the above division between Christ and Adam would imply. Yet, whilst retaining strongly the corporate concept of the Church, even as it appears only dimly in our denominationalism, we suggest that the transfer from one body to another, and particularly from one body separated from others to one more obviously united in itself, allows this admission of the principle of individual action at the point of transfer. We do not say it must be done this way, we merely say it is permissible. We strongly hope that this particular novel proposal will not run into pettifogging opposition.

TYPES OF ACCESSION: (I) THE MISSION CONCEPT

The obvious place to start such a united Church is in the new mission areas. Totally new towns are being built—well then, let the existing denominations which can agree in the sort of bases for union set out earlier launch their union in the new towns. Whole unchurched mission areas could be handed over to the embryonic new Church (detaching them from the Church of England's parochial system by the Act of Parliament which gave powers to inaugurate the union). The negotiating denominations would be sponsors and supporters of the new Church, but their role in relation to it would be that of supporting Churches in England in relation to younger Churches overseas. Such younger Churches have grown from mission control to full independence, and such is exactly the pattern we would envisage for the creating of a united Church in England—it would be the Churches' joint mission into new areas, growing into a fully autonomous and independent Church. This pattern will prove a suggestive starting-point for a consideration later of finance, appointment of ministers, choice of bishops, and a host of other matters. For the moment we would point out that unity-in-mission is not only the easiest starting-point constitutionally for the united Church, but is also theologically crucial to any dynamic concept of the Church and its unity.[1]

In the wake of such allocation of new town areas to the united Church, a further set of accessions would occur in the existing new estates where shared buildings, and sometimes shared worship, give a natural lead towards full integration. Here the relevant local bodies would unite into an organic whole at the point of transfer into the united Church, but the upheavals might not be very great if progress in this direction was already being made. There would, on the other hand, be great gain. At the moment such united or half-united congregations impale themselves on the horns of a dilemma—the more they unite on the local scene, the more they become de facto independents. The lack of a larger framework into which they can fit means that even the most doughty connexionalist is a congregationalist willy-nilly. If, on the other horn of the dilemma, they retain their denominational loyalties, they defeat their ends in uniting and actually thrust upon growing children and new converts the necessity to decide to belong to one or another denomination, the existence of which seems to be unrealistic in the uniting situation. Let these congregations then accede to the united Church and take their place in its growth. There would be relatively few problems here.

[1] See ch. 3, p. 63 above.

TYPES OF ACCESSION: (2) EXISTING DENOMINATIONAL CONGREGATIONS

There are hundreds of areas in which one Church (usually the Church of England) serves a community without any other denominational body competing. In such places these congregations (with the consent of the proper parties) should be able to accede to the united Church. This would again involve the withdrawal by all the parent denominations from any right or responsibility to open up a denominational work there. There is also the more typical mixed church situation. In such cases the united Church would accept no accessions without a local plan for unity being implemented at the same time. Thus, if a local Anglican and Methodist congregation wanted to join the united Church, they would in many cases simultaneously have to join each other in a local organic union. The negotiations for this would obviously include the constitutional framework of the united Church, but would also have to include a rationalization of the local church situation. At this stage the trustees (presumably the bishop and his advisers) of the united Church would have to vet the planning. If they were not satisfied, they would not accept the accession, and the two congregations would have to remain in their traditional denominational positions. A very high level of agreement in the congregations would be requisite before a plan was implemented, so that at no stage would uniting prove divisive.

THE PROCEDURE FOR ACCESSION

The different types of accession set out above would have slightly different ways of implementation. The mission areas would be simply handed over by cession to the united Church with a paper transaction, if they were merely fields on which new houses were being built. The shared Churches, the uniting congregations, and the one-congregation-to-one-place types of accession would be implemented in the course of a liturgical service, with the bishop of the united Church's diocese presiding at a celebration of Holy Communion. Thus the bishop would not only literally and personally receive every acceding congregation at the point of accession, he would also bring each communicant into immediate communion with himself at the point of accession. The fact that in many cases the occasion would see the union of two previously separate congregations, a union through local reconciliation, would heighten the importance of accession being implemented in the course of Holy Communion under the auspices of the bishop. Once this procedure was granted it would be easy to hold on to the double truth expressed in ch. 3 that initiation should be once-for-all (and baptism in water alone would suffice as the initiatory qualification for communion), but that the continuing communicant life of the Church should be focused in the person of the bishop. "Coming into communion with the bishop" would not be an arbitrarily imposed "second initiation"; it would be a simple description of what was happening in the accession service. Those missing on accession day would be expected to come into direct communion with the bishop at his next visit, and on that understanding could remain communicants in the intervening period.

THE RESULT

These different sorts of accession to the united Church should give it a slow, though steady, growth over the whole country. Its basis would be territorial, though with a far more flexible character than the uniform existing Anglican parish. Its congregations would themselves be sometimes "mission" churches, in process of growing to local maturity, sometimes "established" church areas. The former areas would be changing their status to the latter and, whereas shared-church situations are described above as "mission" areas, they would normally have reached "established" status before transfer to the united Church. Thus, their own congregations would be involved in the decision to transfer, and they would play their full part as mature congregations in the united Church.

10

Ministry in the United Church

The ministers of the united Church we have sketched out would be bishops, presbyters, and deacons, with invariable episcopal ordination and consecration practised within the Church. We see considerable need for remodelling the existing concepts of ministry for these particular orders, and as union is by definition *the* time for change, we set out a programme here which is related to the structural and constitutional needs of the united Church.

THE BISHOP

The bishop's office must be conceived of as fulfilling those roles set out in ch. 4 above, and all our proposals are directed to that end. His functions are, briefly, fourfold: the focusing of the unity of the Church within his diocese, the sharing in the episcopate of the Church universal to focus *its* unity, the sustaining and overseeing of the ministry within his diocese, and the pastoral and governmental tasks arising from his position within his diocese.

The episcopate might well be formed by the consecration of the first bishop at the point of cession to him of the first new area for mission along with presbyters and what infant Church could be gathered in that area. His consecration (which might well not be by exclusively *Anglican* bishops) would then set him and his diocese on the task of mission simultaneously, and in the right theological relationship to him. Thus logically and chronologically Church would not precede bishop, nor bishop Church—an exact mirroring of the theological position.

His task thereafter would be initially little concerned with being bishop to his one area (which would of itself not be very demanding of a bishop), but rather with negotiating the continuing accessions and cessions which could be expected. Immediately the job became too big, it would be time for the diocese to divide. Indeed, it would probably be best to ensure that the whole of England should include *four* embryo dioceses at the earliest possible stage of the uniting process. Thus a skeletal General Synod could be formed, the outline of a province set up, and provision made for the consecration of further bishops by those within the episcopate of the united Church. The choice of the first four bishops would lie with the original negotiators, and they would be named in the Act of Parliament setting up the uniting process. Thereafter some joint form of appointment would have to be found—perhaps by nominations coming for ten years from the parent Churches, during which time they would be confirmed by General Synod (hardly by the diocese, as such nominations would usually be at the point of inaugurating a new diocese). For the next ten years nominations might originate within the united Church and be confirmed by the parent Churches. Finally an internal machinery would be worked out and employed.

The basic point of departure in the structures of the new Church would be the concept of the expanding and dividing diocese. The reform of the episcopate should mean that the top limit for the size of a diocese should be about seventy-five[1] congregations, perhaps less. Thus each of the original four dioceses would divide once it passed this figure, if not before, and the process would continue. There would be no hierarchy of dignitaries between the bishop and the ministers of the congregation, and all possible advisory officials (such as architects, administrators, etc.) would be positioned at provincial level, not diocesan. There would be no diocesan cathedrals, or plant, other than a bishop's house. The bishop would be a pastor to his growing flock without great difficulty, but he would have to be a man of considerable vision and energy as he conducted relations with the parent bodies which were slowly ceding their members into the life of the united Church. He would be able to live sufficiently close to his flock to play his full part in initiation.

For the purposes of synodical self-government this sort of diocese would have two distinct advantages: not only could it divide at will, and change its boundaries by simple discussion with its neighbours; it would also fit easily into the framework the nation would ultimately provide for it. If the united Church's expected ultimate size were 12,000 congregations, this would mean 160 dioceses of 75 congregations each, or on a realistic assessment

---

[1] This of course would both fulfil our ideals for the bishop's office, and by the same token exclude the need for suffragan bishops.

nearer 200 of less than 75. If these were in turn to be grouped into 10 provinces of about 20 dioceses each, at each level good representation of the level below would be easy. Proportional representation could be employed to ensure that whatever *de facto* comprehensiveness emerged in the united Church could be faithfully reproduced throughout the levels of decision-taking. This, however, is to look decades into the future.

THE PRESBYTER

The initial presbyters of the united Church would of course have a background of ministry in the various parent bodies. We have shown above (p. 117) that in such a situation we would think it proper to take existing ministers into the episcopally ordered structure with a full acceptance of them as presbyters, with a sending of them to their various ministries by the bishop, and without any possibility of a Pledge being invoked against them.

For each congregation or congregations transferred as "established" churches the initial presbyters would have to be named in the scheme under which the transfer would occur. The scheme would of course be negotiated by the local churches involved, and they would therefore need to participate fully with the representatives of their parent denominations and the bishop of the united Church in making this choice. It is clear that in some areas three or four ministers might serve local denominational congregations and that a union of congregations would make some of the ministers redundant. In such a case delicate negotiation would be required, and progress might be sometimes delayed till a vacancy occurred for other reasons. In other cases ministers sensitive to the situation might well ask their parent denominations for guarantees of appointment when the time of accession came. The negotiating procedures would have to ensure both that a single minister could not frustrate a wholehearted local desire for union, and also that congregations and parent denominations were sensitive to the needs of ministers whose task was disappearing before their eyes. Indeed, lest unions suggest a takeover by one minister or another, there would probably be cases in which all existing ministers found other spheres for ministry and the first united Church appointment of a presbyter was of some other man entirely. The need for care on this point has been aired here, but we add that we are sure that little trouble need be caused if care is observed.

A shared ministry of several presbyters (and of paid and unpaid ones) would be a possible constitutional change, and this would be particularly appropriate to the "mission" areas—which would not have the present sort of parochial boundaries in them. Presbyters entering the united Church ministry from outside, or being ordained within it, would assent to the appropriate confession of faith, profess canonical obedience to the constitution of the united Church and to their own bishop, and receive written authority to fulfil their ministry[1]—all of which might well take place in the initial service of transfer of the area or congregation.

Appointments to ministry thereafter would best be made by one of two methods. In the "mission" area, the diocese, and especially the bishop, would hold responsibility for sending ministers to spearhead the task of building up a Church. In "established" church areas there ought to be much greater participation by the local church in the choice of a minister than is commonly the case in the Church of England today. Here a system of Ministerial Appointment Committees[2] would sit under the chairmanship of the bishop. They would include representatives of the congregation, and some representation of the wider Church. For a number of years (or perhaps better, for a specified number of appointments) this latter element would be provided by representatives of the parent denominations (including, in the case of the Church of England, the existing patron). Later the parent denomination's representation would be replaced by wider representation from the province or from other provinces within the united Church.

After some years men would start to seek ordination within the united Church. There would be no difficulty about this, and the mission character of the united Church might lead many of the best ordinands in the parent Churches to seek a united Church sphere of ministry. It would appear that such men would have a ministry fully recognized and accepted by all the original contracting denominations in England, and for this reason also ministry

[1] Compare the procedure set out on pp. 121–2 above.
[2] Avowedly based on a transitional plan proposed by R. C. Craston for the Church of England in *Patronage Reformed for the Seventies* (Northwood Christian Book Centre 1969).

in the united Church might prove attractive. It is indeed possible, perhaps likely, that ordinands from the non-episcopal Churches would begin to fall into two groups: those who were happy to be ordained by bishops and were so ordained, and those who were totally opposed to the very existence of bishops, let alone their ordinations. This would tend in turn towards the gathering into the united Church of all sympathetic ministers, whilst leaving outside those who were opposed to episcopacy. It is probable, however, that the number of the latter seeking ordination in, say, the Methodist Church would fall rapidly from its present fairly low level.

The presbyter would have tasks and powers defined by the constitution of the united Church. They would include teaching, celebrating the sacraments (both sacraments being equally the presbyter's task[1]), and general pastoral oversight and leadership in the congregation. His relationship to the congregation would depend upon the constitutional arrangements for the lay leadership and responsibility in the congregation (quite apart from questions arising from team ministries), and we are not ready to offer a quick solution to this question. We merely assert that this constitutional relationship (at least in "established" congregations) must protect his tasks and powers as set out above, whilst giving fullest possible expression to the responsibility of the whole local Church for ordering its own life.

We have advised above[2] that it would be impossible to launch in the immediate future a union that accepted the ordination of women to the presbyterate. Accordingly women ministers in some denominations would find themselves unable to join the ministry of the united Church. A similar (though presumably less lasting) situation would obtain where different minimum ages for the ministry were observed. The united Church would need its own rules, and, although it would accept into its ministerial ranks those who had been ordained under its required age, yet it would not do so until they reached that age.

---

[1] Though the bishop would still be the *chief* minister of both, as we have outlined.

[2] See pp. 87–8 above. It would of course be possible for the united Church, on mature conviction and after full consultation with its parent bodies, to change its rules after inauguration, or even to have a pluriform situation varying from one diocese to another.

THE DEACON

The historic or traditional role of the deacon in the threefold order of ministry was to assist the bishop (later the presbyter) in his specifically liturgical ministry. The united Church would have two possible approaches to the problem of the deacon's role in view of the uncertainties and difficulties it occasions today. The Church could either think through a long-term remodelling before inauguration, and follow this pattern from the start, or it could temporarily accept the Anglican concept of one year's probation for the presbyterate whilst talking through jointly with the Church of England a simultaneous remodelling. We do not think that a great deal hangs on this question and we have no necessary preconditions to make. We merely hope that the review would be done at some stage, but it is not crucial when. A similar hope would cover the office of lay reader and other offices.

11

Relations with Other Churches

It is obvious that a growing united Church of the sort we have described would have constant "border problems" with its neighbours. The neighbours would be of two sorts: those who were technically parent denominations, and those who had not been party to the inauguration of the union. Some further brief consideration of the various relationships this situation would involve is here offered.

THE GENERAL STRUCTURE OF RELATIONSHIPS

It is probable that each local Council of Churches, or other similar gathering, would have to sponsor a "parent" committee of the denominations involved in union, with observers from the other local denominations. This committee would be the equivalent of a missionary society's home organization—negotiating the sending of further forces to the young Church and taking a large initial responsibility for its actions and direction. The opposite number of each committee would be the united Church bishop (or sometimes bishop-designate) and representatives of the local congregations involved in reunion. The actual demarcation of powers would require that the parent denominations had a large say in the initial stages of moving towards union, retained some defined relationship with the new congregations as they emerged, and kept residual powers (as suggested in the last chapter) in the appointment of ministers. At a higher level the parent denominations would retain large responsibility in the sphere of finance far past union, would have reserve powers in relation to constitutional changes for a stated number of years, and would have some say (also for a limited period) in the nomination of bishops. Thus the "missionary society" concept would be a very close parallel to the form of union we envisage.

RELATIONS WITH PARENT NON-EPISCOPAL CHURCHES

The two most obvious candidates for inclusion in the early stages of the sort of union described would be the Methodist Church and the future "Reformed" Church (combined Presbyterian and Congregational). There might be other smaller denominations (such as the Wesleyan Reform Union and the Countess of Huntingdon's Connexion) which would be involved, though in most places they would not have representatives; but it is fairly certain that the opponents of infant baptism and rigid congregationalists would have great difficulty in taking part. The official position of the united Church towards the bodies involved would be that they were all acceptable as participating partners in local unions (or new mission areas), their ministers as presbyters, their communicants (provided they were baptized, which would be essential) as communicants. This would mean that the parent Churches in turn would almost certainly grant the same recognition to those ministers and laypeople who moved from the united Church back into an existing denomination. It would not, however, amount to the official conferring by the Church of England of "full communion" status on non-episcopal Churches, and the prospect of the coming into existence of a united Church on an episcopal basis could not be taken as evidence that either the Church of England or the united Church was thereby committed to what the dissentients in the Intercommunion report called "the sufficiency of ecclesiastical structures separated from the episcopate".[1] Thus, when two of us have written that we keep open the question of whether intercommunion before union might be possible officially,[2] we can now make it clear that we refer this to the local situation obtaining after a local scheme for union has been agreed and prior to the actual consummation of union. The Anglicans in such a situation (if it were to happen) would justify the practice at the official level on the grounds that the new local ecclesiology was the determining factor, not the old Anglican one. It would not have any direct implications about Anglican recognition of non-episcopal ministries in their own non-episcopal setting.[3] But equally the present lack

---

[1] *Intercommunion Today*, p. 128, para. 225.

[2] See Appendix 3, pp. 180–1 below.

[3] To this extent the speech attributed to Prebendary Timms by the *Church Times* of 10 October 1969 completely missed our point.

of official ruling on the question of Anglicans receiving communion at non-episcopal celebrations of Holy Communion would presumably continue, and we would urge that such should be the stance of the united Church also. Thus individual liberty of action could not be taken as an official church stance, any more than refusal to avail oneself of the liberty could be.

RELATIONS WITH THE PARENT CHURCH OF ENGLAND

The first and most basic requirement in the relationship between the Church of England and the united Church is that nothing the united Church saw fit to do would of itself bind the Church of England. Thus, no necessary change in any of the Anglican canons or constitutional requirements would be involved. The only point at which a change might arguably be happening would be that the territorial spread of the Church of England would be diminishing by degrees. This would not of itself be fatal to any Anglican principle (it last happened in 1920 when the Welsh dioceses were disestablished and formed into an independent province), and it is obviously a question in a quite separate category from what the internal rules of the Church of England should be.

The process by which the territory of the Church of England would shrink would lead to various questions about the structure of the Church of England itself. There would in time come a point at which diminishing dioceses were amalgamated when vacancies occurred, unless the Church of England itself took advantage of its diminishing size to remodel its own concept of diocesan episcopacy.

A crucial point *vis-à-vis* the Church of England would be boundaries. Whereas areas "ceded" would have only rough boundaries as far as other Churches were concerned, with the Church of England they would have to be marked out very exactly. With weddings, baptismal questions, and a host of others, the boundaries would need to be known. The Act of Parliament permitting the coming into being of the united Church would have to devise a simple method of dealing with boundary changes from the Church of England side.

It seems certain that Church of England bishops and presbyters would be fully acceptable in the united Church where they wished to serve, and the same would be true of bishops and episcopally ordained presbyters *vis-à-vis* the Church of England. There might indeed arise a situation where Anglican presbyters were selected as united Church bishops, and united Church bishops were in turn translated back into Anglican ones.

As to lay communicants, there should be little difficulty, though it would be *just* possible for an exclusive policy to be pursued by the Church of England towards the unconfirmed. The trends within the Church of England, however, suggest that this would be highly improbable. Indeed, the existing Convocation resolutions on relations with South India (dating from 1955) do not treat episcopal confirmation as crucial for communion, and these resolutions are the nearest parallel to what would be required when the united Church was inaugurated.

If there proved to be Anglican lay communicants in a united Church area who had scruples about receiving communion from united Church presbyters, they would require no treatment different from those of one churchmanship who currently find themselves in an area solidly of another sort—they would simply have to accept it or travel on Sundays to a more congenial place of worship. This is a requisite part of the arrangement, and if there proved to be a great need for a continuing Anglican worship centre in any town, it would have to remain (presumably with some parish area) whilst the rest of the area became solidly united Church territory around.[1] This, however, is to offer safeguards which we cannot conceive would be much needed—it might take decades for areas to "go solid", and by that time there would be few, if any, Anglicans unwilling to partake of communion at the hands of united Church presbyters.

RELATIONS WITH OTHER CHURCHES IN ENGLAND

The greatest problem this process would face would be the persistence of denominations which were not party to the uniting arrangement. The dilemma in which this places us is that, if various denominations are not involved, then they may exist alongside united Church congregations and call in question the concept of "one church in each place" which is the basis for union. Equally, it would be impossible to wait for broad agreement in

---

[1] In theory the same situation might arise in hospitals, schools, the Armed Forces, and other non-parochial ministries. In practice we should expect most of these to be able to accede to the united Church easily.

doctrine with Roman Catholics and Baptists before starting the uniting process (for this might delay inauguration up to another thirty years or more). Finally, it would be absurd to *repeat* the process—launching a second united Church to swallow up both the existing one and the Roman Catholics, etc., whilst the first one was still swallowing up the original denominations. This would be to expose us to the same sort of *reductiones ad absurdum* which the Service of Reconciliation is liable to produce.

If we reject this unhelpful set of alternatives, then we must lay out some rough principles for dealing with these bodies. In the first place, they must be involved in the constitution-drafting before inauguration. At every point the doctrinal stand of the united Church must offer the greatest encouragement to other denominations to join the union in principle at a later stage—indeed, it should be a goad, challenging other denominations to declare whether they are really so opposed to the united Church's public stance. Secondly, it must be clear to them that, even when they hold doctrinal agreement with the united Church, yet their congregations can only be received one by one, and then only by negotiating local unions with the relevant diocese of the united Church at the point of transfer. (It would be interesting to know the reaction of English Roman Catholics to this suggestion, both now and in five and in ten years' time.) Thirdly, where a denomination is a federation of autonomous independent congregations (such as the Baptists), then, even where no denominational agreement to the scheme of union has been obtained, every effort will be made to include each local congregation in each relevant round of negotiations.[1] Fourthly, although we would like to see a clear picture emerging of one church in each place, yet we would not be party to any dictatorial attempts to keep non-unionists out of new town areas, and similar developments.

[1] There are Baptist congregations nowadays which do not totally exclude the propriety of infant baptism (though they stress its undesirability), and others not totally opposed to connexionalist patterns of church life and government. Where these two features are found in conjunction, there might be good hope of involving single local congregations in schemes for local organic unity piecemeal without the full weight of their denomination lying behind them (and they *are* autonomous). In such cases special decisions would have to be made about ordained ministers serving in such congregations.

RELATIONS WITH CHURCHES OVERSEAS

Schemes for reunion are far advanced in many countries round the world. The relationship the united Church ought most thoroughly to pursue should therefore be a fraternal one with the united Churches springing up elsewhere. If the existing denominations in England could transfer to the united Church responsibility for support of such Churches overseas at the point at which unions occurred, then it is likely that the overseas commitments of the united Church would grow roughly at the same rate as the Church itself. This might produce a highly pluriform situation. Anglican parishes already supporting the work of the Church of South India would find that they were asked to contribute and support via the united Church's missionary office. Similarly, congregations which joined the united Church, but were already committed through denominational bodies to support for Christian work in areas where the Churches had *not* united, would find that they were in the anomalous position of being united themselves, but of supporting denominational work elsewhere through denominational societies in England. This would all come out in the wash; we merely warn now that pluriformity and permissiveness must be accepted.

The nature of "fraternal relations" with overseas Churches would be hard to forecast. Concordats or relations of "full communion" could not be based on the doctrinal unity which we advocate for organic union in England. Nevertheless, we would hope that support by gifts, prayer, and personnel for the overseas Churches would at least seek a convergence in faith as the backdrop for a discharge of sheer Christian duty.

12

Secondary Matters

There are a whole host of further questions which would need answers in the production of a scheme along the lines outlined in the preceding chapters. In relation to them we have felt ourselves impaled on the horns of a dilemma. On the one hand we might omit treatment of them, and run the risk of future critics seizing on, say, finance, as a secondary matter which would "obviously" be fatal to our scheme. From the standpoint of that risk we had to include all the detail we could think of. Alternatively, if we attempted to fill in the details, we might run the risk of mixing the inessential with the essential, exposing ourselves to the criticism that we had bogged ourselves down in a morass of minutiae, had acted as cardboard experts in every field of church life, and had in any case failed to cover all the necessary ground, so that our omissions were still sinister in their implications. Hidden rocks were still there for the assiduous critic to find.

We have attempted to lift ourselves from this unpleasant impaling by offering *possible* lines of approach to *some* secondary matters. These are offered not as integrally necessary to the type of scheme we have advocated, but simply as some evidence that we are not wholly unrealistic about secondary matters, and we can provisionally see at least one way out of any difficulties they may present us. Others may see other better ways. If so, we would welcome it. We believe that other problems not covered here would also yield fairly easily to determined assault.

CHURCH AND STATE

We would anticipate that the Church of England's role in the nation would remain unchanged for many years after inauguration. There would be no need for the united Church to imitate that role (which in the processes of history is in any case probably in its twilight stages), but there would be time for the united Church to sort out its own relationship with the State as it grew. Initially it might inherit the marriage provisions of the present Church of England in the areas that acceded to it, but not much else. In time it would provide chaplains to various academic and other institutions. But in governmental terms, it would simply govern itself. We can see no role in this for Parliament, except that which it already has in respect of the Free Churches and the Church of Rome. We have already discussed the appointment of bishops, and would not expect the monarch to have any part in it. Ceremonial duties would remain the business of the Church of England primarily, though some growing place for the united Church would have to be found. For this reason some symbolic role for the Crown in relation to the united Church might well be sensible, and should be continued as long as the Christian character of the monarchy is officially maintained.

WORSHIP

The worship of the united Church would not and could not be subject to the concept of uniformity. Some initial agreement on sacramental and ordination services would have to precede inauguration, but non-sacramental services should allow great liberty to the local congregation (which is being treated as mature throughout our thinking). We do not anticipate that those fields in which agreement would be needed would prove intractable in the attempt, and we note the widespread acceptance that the recent Anglican–Methodist Ordinal won, let alone the gentle convergence of thought on eucharistic liturgy which seems to be manifesting itself around Christendom. In any case agreed texts would only be commended rather than imposed, and by some constitutional machinery it would be perfectly possible to conserve existing uses where desired. The need for new texts would particularly arise on central (e.g. diocesan) occasions, and anywhere where worshippers of differing liturgical backgrounds were uniting and wished to transcend their previous differences. But even where existing uses *could* be conserved, the change to the united Church would be well marked by the outward change of adopting the new texts of the united Church. For ourselves, we would expect and desire that the practice of making Holy Communion central to Sunday worship would deepen and grow within the united Church.

FINANCE

It would be easy to assert that the proposals made would be hard
to finance, and it is impossible to show that they would be easy.
There are too many unknowns for any sure thinking to be done.
There are, however, certain good pointers arising from the previous
chapters which would suggest that this should not be too great
a hurdle. Administratively each diocese would be paying only its
stipendiary presbyters and its bishop. There would be no intermediate diocesan officials (such as suffragans, archdeacons, and
dean). The necessary experts (such as architects, financiers, etc.)
would be located at a provincial level. Thus the salary structures
might be fairly economical. Buildings should also give opportunity
for economies. The united Church would not need diocesan cathedrals, and existing cathedrals would remain with the Church of
England for many years after inauguration. In many areas the
local unions would result in having redundant buildings for sale,
and it would have to be a condition of such unions that at least
a portion of such capital gains would go to the central trustees of
the united Church for new building or other capital investment.
But although this elimination of duplication and streamlining of
structures would offer good promise of viability in time, yet the
initial burden would fall upon the parent denominations. The
whole concept of a joint missionary society dictates financial support, though of a type diminishing over the years. This money
would have to be handed over without "strings" in order to reflect
the mutual trust between parents and daughter which must betoken
relationships. The money involved would not need to be new
money, raised over and above existing budgets. It would simply
be the money in existing budgets earmarked for extension work in
new areas, or for ministerial incomes in existing areas. The whole
point would be to redirect existing money (with a view to saving
ultimately), and there should be no general overall increase in costs.

OTHER ADMINISTRATIVE MATTERS

Earlier chapters have already touched on synodical government,
appointments to ministry, missionary and overseas support, and
a host of other things. The question of ministerial training would
also arise, and some standardization of training for those to be

ordained in the united Church would be required. Nevertheless, the existing denominational colleges should do the training for the first decade or more (during which it would be uncertain where or not a man joining a college was going to be ordained in the united Church), and the question of transfer or changeover of colleges could then arise in its natural place. It does not need to be tackled at the outset. This is in turn typical of many other administrative questions which could arise. We have not had time to discuss them, and we cannot but view them as peripheral in importance.

13

Objections Answered

It would of course be easy to think up details which a brief essay could not discuss, and allege them as fatal to such a scheme. The only way to cope with sniping of this sort is dialogue with interested parties, and in time the calling in of expert help (especially legal and drafting help) to find the way through alleged obstacles. We would welcome such dialogue, because we feel it is the only way to get such a scheme right. We have stated all along that a group sitting on the subject can draft only tentatively, and must enter into dialogue with the Churches at all levels.[1] Hence, however destructive detailed criticism might intend to be, our hope would be that it could be turned to constructive use with the adaptation of the details here proposed, or with the supply of details here omitted, such as to meet the objections.

Nevertheless, it is not difficult to foresee some of the objections as we write. We have done our best to stand in the shoes of possible critics and weigh up their weightiest points. These we think might well boil down to three, and these three we therefore set out here to meet.

1. *"The constitutional questions would sink the scheme."* On this we just don't know—but we believe our critics cannot know either. The only answer is to try to do the work. And, if the basic principles were agreed first, and then handed to the denominations for discussion, the legal drafting could go on alongside the discussion. The constitutional structures of congregations, dioceses, and provinces would be a big feature here. Ownership of property would be another. The machinery for the discipline of ministers would be a third. And a host more could be mentioned. On each of these in turn we would repeat our earlier statement: that a tentative agreement of limited duration (say ten years) is all that is needed to start the process, and the united Church would be able to take its own decisions thereafter. For first-round drafting the

---

[1] See our May 1969 Statement in Appendix 1, p. 167 below, and our July 1969 Statement in Appendix 2, p. 174 below.

great necessity is the identification of the problems; this would be laborious, but not beyond the wit of man. Some are already listed in the previous chapter. The great virtue our scheme has at this point is that there does not have to be a wholesale winding-up at the same time as the launching of the united Church. Virtually all existing societies, trusts, constitutions, etc., would remain unchanged. This should bring the problem into the realm of the possible—and we refer back to the point made above[1] that these questions are inevitable anyway.

2. *"The whole process would be interminably slow."* This is *just* possible, but not substantial anyway. It would be so slow only if no new mission areas appeared (which is contrary to all the plans for new towns and for rehabilitation on a large scale in existing ones) and if the existence of a united Church failed to prod or excite others. In other words the process would be slow only in a situation where the recent Scheme could never have mustered any desire for Stage Two anyway. If the Churches are as sluggish as that, and are as certain to remain so as that, then no scheme will make a ha'p'orth of difference. This sort of objection could never be a reason for not trying, and we strongly anticipate it would prove a man of straw in the event.

3. *"The process would have dreadful repercussions on the Church of England."* It is clear that the Church of England would be gradually losing its current place in the country to the united Church, but it is not clear that this should be viewed as a competition with the dice loaded against the Church of England. Many a parish priest would be glad to go on working in his congregation, looking forward to the day when local unity could be achieved, or when his congregation could agree on acceding to the united Church. The impossibility of taking all the steps forward at once that one might like does not exhaust a man's energies for the tasks he *can* do, and the opportunity to look forward in hope is a great strength. Others of course will fear the growing of the united Church. They will want the Church of England to stay exactly as it is, with no steps taken by anyone till everyone can take them together. This we deem to be asking too much. The promise to them that they themselves will not be disturbed, and that the constitution of the Church of England will not be dis-

---

[1] P. 129 above.

turbed, is as far as we think it proper to go. If layfolk find on moving house that they are in a united Church area, then they will have to come to terms with it (just as if they had moved to a C.S.I. area in India—or, to put the case more forcibly, to a Baptist one in Pakistan). Alternatively, the motor-car may be able to deliver them each Sunday to an authentic Anglican parish church. Whereas we think it wrong to compel minorities into a union they distrust, we think it equally wrong for minorities to hold the bulk of a Church to ransom. If the recent Scheme erred in the first way, that does not mean that we intend to react into the second. Our whole plan is designed to avoid both Scylla and Charybdis.

There are other matters at stake in the running-down of the Church of England. One obvious one is the position of existing diocesan bishops. They would be free to accept united Church bishoprics, but it is already clear that the plan envisages these as less exalted, less well-paid, and less traditionalist than the existing Anglican practice. It might well be, therefore, that many diocesans would rather stay where they are. As areas acceded to the united Church, the present dioceses might start to be amalgamated, until relatively few remained. It is probable that cathedrals, with their present status in dioceses, their quasi-national character, and their eclectic congregations, might remain in the Church of England to the last.

A special problem would relate to the Archbishop of Canterbury. His place in the Anglican Communion was one of the contributory factors that led Lord Fisher to play corporate reunion coolly. Our plan would enable this focal role of Canterbury to continue for some time ahead. The Archbishop's own base in the Church of England would of course be diminishing once the united Church had come into being. Equally, however, reunion schemes overseas would mean that it was a diminishing Anglican Communion which gathered round him. The international character of what we know as Anglicanism would be reflected in some fraternal alliance of united Churches, a step which would again be inevitable in *any* plan for reunion.

Objections of this sort (which, one fears, might be found more amongst dignitaries than amongst lay communicants) amount to no more than an urging that a plan should take account of conservative-minded fears and find the kindest way to meet them. We cannot of course legislate in advance for the manner in which the last remaining parts of the present Church of England would finally merge into the united Church. We merely affirm that a generation or more would foreseeably have to pass away first, and thus the fears which have to be met are those not of our own critics but of men yet unborn. And perhaps they will prove not fearful at all.

14

Gains Registered

Lastly, we can spell out the gains in such a plan. They fall easily into four categories.

1. There are *theological* gains. These too may be listed in order.

(*a*) There is a clear doctrinal position holding together the united Church, with a depth and breadth of theological agreement which goes far beyond the hitherto adumbrated "minimalist" position.

(*b*) Local unity is treated as fundamental to sacramental unity, and this seems a great advance on the late scheme.

(*c*) Reform is treated as basic to reunion.

(*d*) The concept of episcopacy in relation to the Church is retained, whilst the practice is overhauled to bring it into line with the theory.

(*e*) The unity of the Church is focused in its missionary character.

(*f*) The local congregation is accorded large and wide powers in ordering its own life, and specifically in moving into the real practice of unity.

(*g*) Unity is treated as dynamic, growing, and flexible, thus marching in step with the concept of the Church as *semper reformanda* and with its missionary character and function.

(*h*) The consciences of minorities are scrupulously respected.

2. There are *psychological* and *psephological* gains. Minorities who are *not* being compelled to act contrary to their conscience may paradoxically accept a course voluntarily which, if compelled, would have been contrary to their consciences! Thus, if the recent Service of Reconciliation had been not mandatory, but offered as a voluntary and symbolic seeking for God's grace, it might well have been more popular. And equally in our plan those who are *not* being compelled into the united Church might well be the happier to see it come about. The situation is comparable perhaps to the pacifist contemplating the current position in Northern Ireland. It is a paradoxical, but perfectly plausible, position for

a man to hold when he says, "I could never bear arms myself, but I am mightily relieved the troops have gone in." So there could be many to wish the united Church well who feel they could not themselves take part in it. And, human creatures as we are, the wishing it well *could* be the beginning of being prepared to take part in it later.

The psephological gains come in the wake of the psychological ones. The recent Scheme could not muster the moral unanimity in two Churches which it needed. But this plan would need a totally different sort of voting support. At the centre it could well manage with a smaller vote in favour (even whilst, if the above paragraph is true, it should gain a larger one!). Those who voted against would not be personally squeezed in conscience when the plan was adopted, as on the recent Scheme, and a larger minority could therefore be theoretically tolerated. Perhaps a two-thirds majority at the centre would do.

On the other hand, moral unanimity would be needed at the local level. This stands in stark contrast to the late Scheme. Then only one or two laymen in each parish had any say (even a diocesan conference straw vote) in the decision. If there were odd parishes with more than two (and even rarer parishes with a member of the House of Laity), equally there were many, where elections to diocesan conferences have been made at ruridecanal level, which had no members of the diocesan conference at all. The future of a congregation was virtually beyond their power to influence at all—they were pawns in someone else's game. They were furthermore open to being used surreptitiously as more than pawns—a groundswell in favour of the Scheme was easy to assert in the absence of the requisite display of opinion. And finally it is probable that they were willing to be used as such, for, although a change in the Church of England was at issue, it was not one that would have proved costly in the average parish. Thus the ill-informed could lightly acquiesce in the proposed steps, without there being any obvious immediate local consequences.

Our plan works the other way. For congregations to unite and accede to the united Church they would have to display a single moral will to it, being ready in their own persons to sustain the implications of their decision, the cost, the new ways of church life, the openness to further reform. Every communicant ideally would be involved in the decision, and the guidance of the Spirit would be sought in moral unanimity, without which the implementation would have to be delayed.

Such a plan would provide a far better test of people's seriousness in voting "yes". It is the proper expression of the Church as an organic living body. We are convinced, not only that a plan which distributes the decision-taking in this realistic way is the only one which has any chance of success, we are equally sure that it is the only one which *ought* to have such a chance.

3. There are *practical* gains. These stem from the actual union of local churches. Vast duplications of buildings, employees, paperwork, and other institutionalized secondary features of church life should be able to be eliminated. Slowly there would emerge financial gains also, as the ministerial and other structures devised should prove far cheaper to run.

4. There are *missionary* gains—or might be. We are always told that the Churches must unite in order to make their message credible. We are not wholly convinced of this, but we anticipate that the sort of plan envisaged would make some impact upon the minds of men outside the Church. At least the fact of division would be less easy to allege as excuse for practical atheism, and in many areas the actual uniting of congregations could lead to some liberating of missionary energies. We do not want to put this point too high. We believe that unity should be sought as a reflection of the unity of God, and the results must be left to him. But we do believe that setting up the united Church as in essence a missionary society of the parent denominations can only assist in God's mission, and we venture thus to say so.

Appendixes

The material grouped here is largely backward-looking towards 1969, and is collected here for the sake of the record. The two Statements made by our Group to the Convocations come first. These were the subject of much comment in the Convocations, and led in turn to new discussion between Catholic and Evangelical proctors. The third Appendix was written for *Theology* of October 1969, in preparation for the October 1969 Convocation debate on the report *Intercommunion Today*. In the event the Convocation debate led to little progress. The fourth Appendix takes up a separate theological issue entirely, but is a further paradigm of the procedure we have adopted throughout—a talking through of hard issues together. Although some members of the Group had no part in compiling one or other or both of Appendixes 3 and 4 they carry the general approval of the whole Group.

The fifth, sixth and seventh Appendixes are concerned wholly with the late Scheme. Appendix 5 analyses the Service of Reconciliation not from a Catholic or an Evangelical standpoint, but simply from a logical one. Appendix 6 sets the voting figures out for reference purposes. Appendix 7 lists the previous writings of each of us on the subject of reunion, and invites comparison between what we have individually said in the past and what we say together now. A scrutiny will reveal that we say not exactly the same things, but that the directions were clearly set which would lead to this conjunction. The bibliographies are arranged in chronological order, and for accuracy in the record Appendixes 1 and 2 ought to be incorporated at the appropriate points.

Statement on Anglican–Methodist Unity to the Members of the Convocations of Canterbury and York
May 1969

1. The Anglican–Methodist Unity Scheme stands today as a cause of division in both the Churches concerned. We are told that its rejection would lead to widespread cynicism and despair. We are ourselves convinced that attempts to implement it as it stands would produce greater disruption and harm. Nor do we believe that delaying the decision could be helpful—it would merely deliver the Churches over to an intermediate period of further pamphleteering, posturing, and pressurizing, and to an ultimate decision no less injurious to the two Churches than one this year would be.

2. We are aware that those who favour the Scheme have urged that, because Evangelicals and Anglo-Catholics are so far divided from each other, the combined weight of their opposition to the Scheme (and particularly to the Service of Reconciliation) can be discounted. This argument suggests that any "concession" to Anglo-Catholics would immediately alienate what Evangelical support there already exists for the Scheme, and vice versa. We are unable to feel the force of this defence of the Scheme. We believe rather that the argument is ill-judged and out of accord with the facts, and the resort to it smacks of somewhat panicky expediency. We for our part acknowledge our responsibility to seek agreement with each other, if that is possible, and we now publish this Statement to show how much nearer we stand to each other than any of us does to the Service of Reconciliation. We thus have a good hope that a scheme could be devised which would include us all with a clear conscience. And, if this is so, could not the "centre" of the Church of England go with us?

3. We do not need at this point to reiterate in full our personal and differing objections to the Scheme. They are fully set out

elsewhere. We merely insist that they run very deep in our theological thinking and in our understanding of our personal discipleship of Christ. They are in no way "party"-inspired in the sense that they reflect any group pressures upon us individually. We all believe that our objections would in principle stand unchanged even though the rest of both Churches were unanimously in favour of the Scheme. In particular none of us could participate in the mutual laying on of hands in the Service of Reconciliation. We are agreed that whatever may be the meaning of the Service it does not serve its purpose. It is intended to integrate the ministries. In fact it will produce three sets of Methodist ministers (episcopally ordained, reconciled, and unreconciled). First, the official promise to the "reconciled" that their sacramental ministries will be acceptable to all Anglicans cannot be honoured, and secondly could only be made at all on the official understanding contained in the Anglican Canons that they have, in fact, been episcopally ordained. What we plead is that an ambiguous service which is designed to satisfy both Catholics and Evangelicals and satisfies neither should be dropped.

4. Our personal conscientious reasons for such abstention are now reinforced by the degree of opposition manifested in both Churches. We draw attention to the following points: first that 4216 Anglican clergy have voted that they disapprove of the Service of Reconciliation in the diocesan conferences. This figure is not exhaustive of Anglican clergy, and in the diocese of London alone 350 clergy voted such disapproval at deanery level, of whom only 88 were able to vote at the diocesan conference and to be included in the 4216 cited above. And even the 4216 without such additions is a figure larger than the total ministerial strength of the Methodist Church. Our second point concerns the Methodist circuit voting. Excluding neutral votes, the percentages for individual voting were 54·8% in favour and 45·2% against. For the voting by circuits, the percentages were 58·4% in favour and 41·6% against. The evidence is that few if any Methodists have changed their minds in favour of the Scheme since 1965, though on the admission of all students of the Scheme the shift in its content since 1965 has been perceptibly in favour of Methodist scruples. This is no time to analyse the reasons, theological or non-theological, for such strong continued opposition to the Scheme. The simple fact is that it is

now non-viable and unenforceable. Thus, even if in our own persons we had been in favour of the Scheme, we would now feel that the only responsible course for both Churches was to reject it, and try to find a better way.

5. In speaking of trying to "find a better way" we emphasize our concern for the unity of these two Churches (as indeed of all the Churches in this land). We share the theologically inspired desire to glorify God by the visible reunion of his people which underlies the best forms of ecumenical activity. We therefore profess that we think the Churches should reject the Scheme, but that should not be the end of the matter. No doubt rejection of the Scheme is the first action to be taken in chronological sequence, but if it were taken in isolation it would undoubtedly (and perhaps deservedly) lead to frustration and even recrimination. None of us would feel justified in joining hands across the theological differences which divide us purely to achieve such a negative and hollow result. We believe positively that the Churches must seek a better way, and it is *that* which unites us in this Statement. We are fully aware of the difficulties in finding a way which will do justice to the conscience of each one of us, and enable the Church of England to retain her overall integrity. We make no secret of our belief that possibly no scheme at all may be viable at the moment, so divided internally is the Church of England. But we have good reason for hoping that, given time for the necessary work, based on a consideration of first principles, we personally could all be comprehended in a single scheme for Anglican–Methodist unity. The very fact that there has been no time for such work precludes us from putting forward concrete proposals. It is perhaps relevant to point out that the Scheme which took twelve years to complete has been available for discussion for only one year. In any case, we have been officially discouraged from offering alternatives (even whilst we were told that none could be found).

We are bound by a common belief in the revelation of God in Scripture, and, whilst the exact status of primitive tradition is not agreed amongst us, we are already aware, after some meetings together, of both the distance we all stand from the years 1956–63 (when the present Scheme had its birth) and of the increasing respect we each have for the other's position. We have felt very strongly that further meeting would bring us to a more full-bodied statement of possible ways forward, and we publish now, not because we feel entirely ready to do so, but because we feel the times demand it. We have, as we fully admit, only come together very late in the day. And, as we have said above, we would have anticipated a deeper and more satisfying unity amongst ourselves if we had been able to work and think together for a longer period. We are, in fact, committed to meeting regularly to continue our discussions.

6. We would, however, make the following remarks:

(a) We are ultimately interested in that unity which would join separated congregations into what would be sacramentally and visibly one. We believe that "higher echelon" organizational integration, which might or might not precede the prior aim in point of time, must either squarely serve this aim or be discarded as irrelevant.

(b) We believe that a scheme must not make further unions harder to consummate. The Service of Reconciliation pattern cannot be repeated in future unions, and this means that some other form of ministerial integration must be found at some point in any case. If it can be found now, the long-term thinking towards multilateral reunion will be encouraged, whereas in these terms the present Scheme is a cul-de-sac.

(c) Whilst the problem of integrating ministries has to figure in any outline sketches of possible ways forward, we strongly disavow any suggestion that we consider this the only question at issue in church union. It is a question forced upon us by the existence of key differences at this point, and by the actual solution propounded in the present Scheme. But it is in itself a question which must be considered in the light of those relating to Scripture and tradition, creeds, sacraments, and justification. It is only against the setting of growing together in these spheres that we would want to make any proposals about integrating ministries.

(d) We are united in our preference for a one-stage scheme. The origins of the present Scheme reveal that its two-stage character was a freak of history out of which men have understandably made a virtue. We know the constitutional difficulties in producing a one-stage scheme, and in particular we realize it would take longer to inaugurate. But we would expect that it could be implemented faster than its equivalent, that is Stage Two, can be reached on the present Scheme. Its merit is that it would avoid the risk of indefinitely prolonging the "parallel episcopates" period (during which episcopacy is exposed not only to the distortions in existing Anglican and proposed Methodist practice, but also to the risk of becoming a symbol of disunity instead of unity). It would concentrate minds upon the Stage Two problems which must be faced before real union can be achieved and which we are currently urged not to look at too closely. It would also relate union at the local level more satisfactorily to the administrative integration of the two Churches.

7. In making these remarks, we ask for careful consideration to be given to the following procedural proposals:

(a) Any new commission should have very open terms of reference to explore not only our suggestions, but any others that may arise inside or outside its membership.

(b) Such a commission should have a high proportion of members of deep-rooted theological conviction and concern, covering the full spectrum of such differences as obtain within and between the two Churches.

(c) Such a commission should conduct its business in an "open-walled" way. Thus its members could constantly refer draft proposals to representative groups. This would help the commission to be sensitive to the mind of the Churches, and would help the mind of the Churches to move with the commission's discussions. Only in this way can we avoid the unhappy situation where the work of a few men is placed on the table, hailed as the mind of the Church, and treated as deserving our loyalty purely because those few men have agreed it.

(d) A full range of participating observers from Churches not party to the negotiations should be included.

8. In short we ask the Churches to say a speedy and decisive "no" to the present Scheme, not in order to bury all hopes for unity, but in order to foster and further them. We for our part solemnly attest our concern for the attaining of that unity which our Lord

has commanded to his Church, and we disavow any intention of posturing or prevaricating or of concealing our true aims. It is in that spirit of a clearer determination to serve our Lord that we here "cast our bread on the waters".

COLIN BUCHANAN
MICHAEL GREEN
E. L. MASCALL
J. I. PACKER
✠ GRAHAM WILLESDEN

2 May 1969

A Further Statement on Anglican–Methodist Unity to the Members of the Convocations of Canterbury and York
July 1969

1. On 8 July the Convocations take what is probably their biggest decision since 1661. We make this Statement to the members of Convocation on the eve of that decision to give expression to three matters:

(*a*) We join with the many others in praying that God's name may be honoured and glorified in the decision taken, and that he will give to us that unity which is his will.

(*b*) We wish, in view of some misunderstanding, to clarify our intentions as a group.

(*c*) We draw attention to certain important considerations which bear upon the question as to what course to unity the Church of England ought to pursue.

2. Our Statement of May 1969 was written with utmost seriousness. The origins of our group reach back to the Anglican–Methodist Council for Unity, on which the Bishop and Colin Buchanan met from 1966 to 1968, and to Lambeth 1968, where the Bishop and Michael Green served together. A first meeting for theological discussion as a group was held in October 1968, and a later meeting had to be cancelled through a pastoral emergency. Reconvening did not prove possible until April 1969, and even then not of all of us at once.

Our seriousness in our last Statement committed us to continue. The four[1] signatories of this Statement have spent ten hours together in the last six weeks, and have circulated eight theological documents between meetings. We shall continue to meet after

---

[1] Michael Green has been out of the country during the compilation of this Statement, and is for this reason alone not a signatory. [Original footnote.]

8 July to pursue these theological concerns. We view our existence as a group as neither solely nor even chiefly related to the impending vote on the Scheme.

Our agenda have included lengthy discussions of Scripture and Tradition, of Church and sacraments, and of episcopacy and ministry. We have constantly been driven back to first principles, and, despite the lack of time, have felt it vital to explore at that level as much as at the level of particular proposals. It is true that, feeling the force of the argument that the opponents of the present Scheme are so far divided among themselves that no other Scheme could produce better support, we started with a moral obligation to explore how far this might be so. But our explorations have been directed much more to clarifying and comprehending each other's position than to trying to produce a whole alternative Scheme in a few weeks. We have found our common concern to be not so much to formulate policy in respect of this Scheme as to pursue at the level of theological clarity the cause of the real unity and health of the Church of God.

3. Yet we do not believe that the present Scheme can be implemented. The House of Laity voting and the clergy "referendum" highlight its gravely divisive character. If it were implemented, there might not be that degree of open schism which would be bound to occur in the Methodist Church. Nevertheless, the ensuing division in the ranks of the clergy alone would be appalling. Over one-third of them would have unremittingly uneasy consciences in the new alignment of the Church. Their continued presence would be an embarrassment to the Church. Their departure no one could desire. In any event the unity of the Church of England would be imperilled, perhaps irremediably.

4. On the other hand, we do not believe that a rejection of the Scheme will be admission of total failure on the Church's part (let alone on the Commission's part). It should not take us back fourteen years. The Church will have learned valuable lessons, and the path to a real unity should, we think, be the easier. Above all, there will be opportunity to make theology primary in the new quest.

This shift of emphasis we believe to be vital. It is true that a new Scheme could utilize much of the work done by the recent Commission (e.g. its Ordinal). But our passionate belief in the visible unity of the Church is coloured by an equal belief that it can be sought properly only by and with reform. Because the Church lives constantly under the judgement of God, it should abjure merely pragmatic moves in the name of unity. We conceive the original suggestion that the Free Churches should (in Lord Fisher's words) "try out episcopacy on their own ground" to have been such a false move. Although we applaud the later recognition that this must lead to organic unity, yet that first step, which was by then irretraceable, remained nakedly pragmatic. The resultant Scheme did not proceed from any convictions about the nature of the Church, it did not seek the reform of church structures and patterns of life (which were all postponed), it thus never had a clear eye to the Church's missionary task, and it was unable to focus properly on the sort of unity it hoped to achieve. The particular questions of local unity were not even raised. On these grounds we ask for a return to theology, and we cannot view the rejection of the Scheme as a disaster.

5. A pragmatic understanding of the Church has also unfortunately emerged in the voting procedures for decision. There has been a tendency abroad to spell out the theme "majorities have rights as well as minorities". They do, we concede. They also have duties. But both points are irrelevant. If the Church is indwelt by the Holy Spirit, we ought patiently to look for moral unanimity in great decisions. To decide by majorities is to vitiate our understanding of the divine nature of the Church.

We would point this up by our own resolve. We vary among ourselves in our degree of opposition to the Scheme and in our proposed courses of action if it should be implemented. But we are fully agreed in saying that none of us could vote for a Scheme which would cut another of us out. We believe that the lesson to be learned is that discussion should be "open-walled" with constant reference back to the Churches. This should then lead to a Scheme which is carried by acclamation, which is a proper expression of the Spirit-filled body of Christ.

6. We here sketch out three primary features of a united Church as theological priorities to be considered in any reconstruction. If they proved proper goals, then the steps towards them should

emerge more easily, and the temptation to stop short of them should be diminished. They could become the subject of widespread education whilst they were being first debated in the Churches and finally erected as goals.

(a) The oneness sought should be organic, visible, and sacramental. We firmly believe that the sacraments and the ordained ministry are in principle related to the structures of the Church. Whether another Church becomes episcopal in separation from us or not, this theological principle will not allow that a sacramental wholeness can be achieved without a union of structures, and would only justify sacramental arrangements without such a union as provisional steps leading to it.

(b) The beliefs and practice of the united Church should be controlled by theological norms, with explicit reference to the Bible. The Church must confess its faith in the Christ of the Scriptures, and seek constantly to live under the word of God and to reform its way of life accordingly.

(c) Unity should be visible locally and should be mission-orientated. We have much sympathy with those definitions of the Church which include its mission. It is not just that the Church has missions. Nor even just that the Church has a mission. It is that the Church *is* God's mission on earth. And, if the unbelieving world is to meet God's missionary community (and thereby his message of salvation), it is everywhere the local church it will meet. Because unity is intimately related to local mission, high priority should be given to seeking actual local organic unity—a theme evaded by the present Scheme.

We strongly anticipate that these goals can be brought nearer by the demise of the present Scheme, and that for two reasons. First, the two-stage method has postponed consideration of goals until there should be already some momentum. Thus, if the momentum proved to be in the wrong direction, this would lead to the wrong goals, but even on the best view such a procedure would still cause delay in establishing goals. A one-stage scheme, however, starts from reflection on its goals. Secondly, the present Scheme would have to complete even more Stage One negotiations if other Churches were to be included, and consideration of Stage Two would be further postponed. Again, a one-stage multilateral scheme would avoid this. These factors together suggest that, on a long view, the true goals of union can be identified and brought into sight more quickly by the rejection of the present Scheme. We do not put this point as a *ground* for the Convocations to reject the Scheme. The final decision should now be grounded neither on the Scheme's merits or demerits as individuals see them, nor even on the probable good or ill results of one course or another, but simply on the significance the Convocations attach to all the various rounds of voting. Our point is made only as an alleviation of the undoubted pain involved in rejecting the Scheme.

7. On the short view also we see reason to expect progress without the Scheme. Whatever theological conversations or negotiations may tackle national organic union, the short-term focus is bound to be the local Church. Here we discern three areas in which progress is already speeding up or could imminently do so. These are:

(a) *The Sharing of Churches.* We welcome the Bill now before Parliament and see this, along with the more flexible domestic provisions of the Pastoral Measure and the new mood in liturgical experimentation, as hastening the local unity we desire.

(b) *Intercommunion.* We repeat that sacramental practice is in principle an outworking of the theology of the Church and its structure. We feel the need to explore further how far "intercommunion" can be set in organic relationship to the oneness of the Church understood eschatologically. We shall address ourselves to this task in coming meetings. But meanwhile we draw a distinction between the formal outworkings of an exact ecclesiology, and the sheer fact of the existence of "Free Church" (and indeed Roman Catholic) baptized communicants not only in their separate congregations, but for various reasons often in ours or in shared churches. This distinction is well made in a statement of Vatican II about the Eastern Orthodox, "Divine Law forbids any *communicatio in sacris* which would damage the unity of the Church, or involve formal acceptance of falsehood or the danger of deviation in the faith, of scandal or of indifferentism. At the same time, pastoral experience clearly shows that with respect of our Eastern Brethren there should and can be taken into consideration various circumstances affecting individuals wherein the unity of the Church is not jeopardized nor are intolerable risks involved, but in which salvation and the spiritual profit of souls are urgently at issue" (Decree on Eastern Catholic Churches 26). We recognize that Vatican II acknowledged the validity of Eastern orders and sacraments, but this acknowledgement is only incidental to the formal distinction which concerns us (provided only that we accept other denominations' baptisms). The distinction between formal ecclesiology and somewhat anomalous pastoral practice might well, we think, find disciplinary expression. In saying this we are not here concerned with the *present* rules (about the meaning, authority, and propriety of which we differ somewhat among ourselves), but only with the principles which should guide the making of *future* rules.

(c) *Theological conversations.* The present Scheme's procedures have pre-empted proper theological discussion at the local level. At each stage a ready-made product has been put before the parishes, deaneries, and dioceses, and has been commended on a "this or nothing" basis. But with a clean start it should be possible to involve local communities of Christians much more fully in the work of preparing a Scheme. We visualize that the asking of key theological questions, which would stimulate ecumenical discussion in the context of prayer and mutual love at a local level, could be a most fruitful way of restarting initiatives towards union. As a dialogue opens between the central questioning body and the local groups, so the Churches will move (albeit slowly) towards that unity-by-acclamation which we so much desire to see.

8. Our conversations have often turned to looking for an alternative method of integrating ministries, a method which would win the assent of us all. We know this question looms in the forefront of both Churches' thinking—forced there by its prominence in isolation at Stage One of the Scheme. We are thus well aware of the "political" impact of offering a way of integrating ministries. Nevertheless, we do not do so, simply because we have not reached a point in our rushed agenda where it would be possible. We still profess what we said in our May Statement—"We have felt very strongly that further meeting would bring us to a more full-bodied statement of ways forward." We continue to meet. But we have learned together that we can put forward practical proposals only on the sure foundation of shared theological principles. Were we to do less, we would act out of accord with our own criticisms of

the present Scheme, and would call in question our own seriousness in urging different procedures in future. Were others to put
forward emendations to the present Scheme, any or all of us might
be able to accept them. But we have felt increasingly unable to put
forward ourselves anything that could look like mere tinkering
with the Scheme. Hence, in this particular case, we do not offer
an "Open Sesame" solution to the integration of ministries such
as to suggest that *this* is the minor adaptation we desire. As we
continue to meet we shall hope to publish on the subject later,
in the context of a fuller theological treatment of Church, ministry,
and sacraments.

9. In writing as we do, we claim to represent no one but ourselves
as four individuals. We rejoice at the openness we have discovered
in each other, and we discern similar signs elsewhere in the Church.
We repeat what we said in May that "we make no secret of our
belief that possibly no scheme at all may be viable at the moment"
—but that does not mean that the same will be true in six, eight,
or ten years' time. A one-stage scheme then would be a tremendous
advance on a Stage Two in twice the time. We urge that the work
for this should be put in hand immediately.

COLIN BUCHANAN
E. L. MASCALL
J. I. PACKER
✠ GRAHAM WILLESDEN

5 July 1969

Intercommunion—Some Interim Agreement
August 1969

In the Spring of this year there took shape a group of five Anglican clergy, two Catholics and three Evangelicals,[1] who shared a dismayed concern over the basis and probable effects of the Anglican–Methodist Unity Scheme. The two public statements of this group made it clear that they were united not only in opposing the tabled Scheme, but also in desiring a viable alternative. They had in fact been brought together partly through the criticism that they were so deeply opposed to each other (as well as to the Scheme) that no alternative could be found which would suit them better than the rather rickety Scheme. This seemed to lay a moral obligation on the five to work together, and they are to that extent grateful for the rather provocative criticism which brought home to them their mutual duties. The disappointment which they have since sometimes felt has been due to a predilection in their critics not only to say they could not agree, but to criticize them again for trying to. A little time has now been bought, and the group works on. The common hope of all five is that they might contribute positively to the rebuilding which is now necessary.

At the time of writing only the two signatories of this essay are able to meet, and they alone are responsible for it. They have never viewed intercommunion as the primary problem in ecumenical relations, and to that extent view this as a passing task on the group agenda. The intention is purely to cite, and then to expound, the relevant section of the statement addressed by four[2] of us to the Convocations in July.

[1] Colin Buchanan, E. M. B. Green, Dr E. L. Mascall, Dr J. I. Packer, and the Bishop of Willesden.
[2] The Revd Michael Green was out of the country at the time and for that reason took no part in compiling the second statement.

THE TEXT OF THE STATEMENT

7. On the short view (as well as the long) we see reason to expect progress without the Scheme. Whatever theological conversations or negotiations may tackle national organic union, the short term focus is bound to be the local church. Here we discern three areas in which progress is already speeding up or could imminently do so. These are:

(a) The Sharing of Churches.

(b) Intercommunion. We repeat (from para. 6) that sacramental practice is in principle an outworking of the theology of the church and its structure. We feel the need to explore further how far "intercommunion" can be set in organic relationship to the oneness of the church understood eschatologically. We shall address ourselves to this task in coming meetings. But meanwhile we draw a distinction between the formal outworkings of an exact ecclesiology, and the sheer fact of the existence of "Free Church" (and indeed Roman Catholic) baptized communicants not only in their separate congregations, but for various reasons often in ours or in shared churches. This distinction is well made in a statement of Vatican II about the Eastern Orthodox, "Divine Law forbids any *communicatio in sacris* which would damage the unity of the Church, or involve formal acceptance of falsehood or the danger of deviation in the faith, of scandal or of indifferentism. At the same time, pastoral experience clearly shows that with respect of our Eastern Brethren there should and can be taken into consideration various circumstances affecting individuals wherein the unity of the Church is not jeopardized nor are intolerable risks involved, but in which salvation and the spiritual profit of souls are urgently at issue" (Decree on Eastern Catholic Churches 26). We recognize that Vatican II acknowledged the validity of Eastern orders and sacraments but this acknowledgement is only incidental to the formal distinction which concerns us (provided only that we accept other denominations' baptisms). The distinction between formal ecclesiology and somewhat anomalous pastoral practice might well, we think, find disciplinary expression. In saying this we are not here concerned with the *present* rules (about the meaning, authority, and propriety of which we differ among ourselves), but only with the principles which should guide the making of *future* rules.

(*c*) Theological conversations.

A FORMAL ECCLESIOLOGY

The ecclesial character of Holy Communion is one of the Sacrament's most important features. There is but one baptism for Christians and it is supposed to join men into one Church—one, that is, in its organic internal cohesion in the Lord, and one in its visible external manifestations to the world of a loving community. Particular emphasis is laid in the New Testament upon the Church's oneness locally, and upon its oneness universally. If we are to take St Paul seriously, that oneness, which baptism is supposed to inaugurate, communion is supposed to reflect and sustain throughout the Church's earthly pilgrimage. In principle the practice of communion, and the context within which it is recurrently celebrated, is integrally bound up with the nature of the Church. It is supposed to have boundaries co-terminous with the boundaries of the one organic Church created by baptism. Those within the Church should be regular communicants (not excluding young children entitled to baptism because their families are Christian), and those outside it should not be, until, that is, they have received baptism which in ecclesial terms must be reckoned as receiving Christ and being incorporated into him. There is a continuing problem (which we have frankly not yet discussed between ourselves) as to the status of confirmation in Christian initiation. We discern great uncertainties in the Church of England today as to the age for confirmation, the degree of obligation attaching to it, the proper minister of it, the "grace" of it, the relation between laying on of hands and baptism, the relation between laying on of hands and admission to communion. We can, however, at least register agreement that lack of confirmation does not necessarily imply that sitting lightly to ecclesial structures which lack of baptism or of communion would mean, and similarly it is not necessarily to be equated with that rejection of episcopacy which it certainly signified in the seventeenth century.

All this is easy to state and is apparently close to the New Testament and to patristic thinking. It does, however, still seem remote from the problems which press upon us. The New Testament and the primitive Church do not reveal the same multiplicity of denominations that confront us today; they do not face the same hoary problems about the status of the ministry and of specific kinds of ministries, and they do not exhibit catholics and evangelicals trying to agree with each other! We frankly find it hard therefore to work simply from the common ground set out in the last paragraph, because we stand within or near our own respective traditions and have difficulty in being objective. In so far, however, as we can get outside our traditions, we would venture the following self-criticisms. Catholics have been far too concerned with clerical pedigree in itself, and insufficiently sensitive to the need to root the standing of the celebrant in the structure of the Church as a locally manifest community. Evangelicals have been in reaction against this and have been too concerned with the "one-to-one" standing of the communicant before God, to the exclusion of most if not all ecclesiological questions. The upshot has been that both sets could in certain circumstances acquiesce in two or more competing communion tables on one street corner. Evangelicals would in this century have been largely concerned with whether the individual was converted, and, once granted that, any or all communion tables would be viewed as "the Lord's Table" not ours, and therefore open to all believers. Catholics would have wanted guarantees about the episcopal ordination of the celebrant at both (and possibly of the episcopal confirmation of the communicants) but, once granted that, might have been relatively happy for the two congregations to continue side by side. (Indeed, although the Anglican–Methodist Scheme proposed to eliminate parallel episcopates at Stage Two, it still did not breathe a word about unifying congregations likewise—so to that extent the idea that a mere straightening out of clerical pedigrees would suffice has persevered to the present day.) We think both these strong traditions represent an inadequate ecclesiology, and would urge that a stated intention of returning to the "one church in each place" pattern of the New Testament should be a foundation feature of all schemes.

This critique of our own traditions outlines certain problems—it does not solve them. But in terms of practice we can well see several different disciplines might be regarded as attempts to approximate to the ideal in the world of the madly ramified denominations. We can spell these out:

(i) To restrict communion to one's own denomination, as the Lutherans usually do, may not be so much to condemn all other Christians as to erect the ideal of one church co-terminous with its own communicants.

(ii) To practise completely indiscriminate communion and inter-communion is to take others seriously in their claim to be Christians and to take their communions seriously, as being truly the Lord's instituted ordinance.

(iii) To practise open communion towards others, whilst hesitating oneself to visit "their" communions, may be a combination of (i) and (ii) above—i.e. a holding to the ideal of one Church and one communion in each place, but using the sacrament as a means of helping to gather the one Church.

Now it is clear at sight that each of the strengths of these views has equal and opposite weaknesses. But whereas (i) and (iii) clearly do hold to an ecclesiological ideal, it is less certain that (ii) does. However, they are all attitudes of one particular denomination or of one group of people—they are in a sense all slightly defensive stances towards ecumenical problems. It is a question whether there are circumstances in which the ecumenical situation warrants *reciprocal* arrangements going beyond either (i) or (iii) and justify-ing themselves ecclesiologically as not being (ii) *simpliciter*.

AT OR BEFORE UNION?

View (i) above represents no intercommunion before union. View (iii) unilateral open communion with a view to union. There is a pressure nowadays for a "covenant" as a context for intercom-munion between specified "covenanting" Churches. We are un-persuaded about the "covenant", for, if it means a commitment to seek union, it is no more than the articulate public stand that most of the historic Churches currently take. This might, there-fore, be a cheap public move for several Churches to take which proved in effect merely to bring them into category (ii) above, and apparently *further* from the ecclesiological ideal. It might be of some significance to cite against this the public statement of all the Anglican bishops in the South Indian dioceses in 1946: "After the inauguration of Union we, as Bishops of the Church of South India, shall be ready ourselves to receive communion at the hands

of any Bishop or Presbyter of the United Church."[1] This statement was made, of course, to hearten the non-episcopalians as to
the treatment they would receive in a united episcopal Church. But
it is significant that the bishops were *not* prepared to make the
gesture then in 1946 (i.e. before the inauguration of union). This
was not because of scruples about the propriety of celebration by
non-episcopal ministers, for they would receive from such men
after union. No, they were restrained not by Apostolic Succession,
but by ecclesiology. The relation of communion to structures of the
Church was something important to them—and they were largely
of a C.M.S., not a High Church, background. It is perhaps at least
as significant that the evangelical bishops were not prepared to
advertise their willingness generally to receive communion from
non-episcopal ministers *before* union as it is that the one S.P.G.
bishop (Michael Hollis) was prepared so to receive *after* union.
Far back behind this statement lay the careful resolution of the
Episcopal Synod of the C.I.B.C. in 1932 which permitted intercommunion as an exceptional practice in a situation where it was
clear that unity would result (and on the negotiating committee),
but added "In giving this liberty the Synod would emphasize the
fact that it cannot believe that general intercommunion before
union is the right way of working for unity." The interest about
this today is that the resolution was opposed by Catholics from
Archbishop Lang downwards, and was passed by a combination
of Evangelicals and moderates.

This Indian resolution will help to show that ecclesiology need
not rule out the possibility of a degree of intercommunion by
agreement before the consummation of a union. The resolution
held firmly to the importance of structures and context.

Thus, whereas we deem the cloudy concept of a "covenant" as
not sufficiently near to a grappling with the question of structures,
we might not want to take the same view of a period after decisions were taken on specific plans and schemes, but before the
actual union was inaugurated. Here there might be a good case, as
there would also be a strong lay instinct, for a degree of sacramental relationship which was related logically to the impending
union, and only anticipated it in point of time because the ecclesiology justified it.

[1] Bengt Sundkler, *The Church of South India* (Lutterworth 1954), p. 321.

FURTHER CASES: (I) LOCAL ECUMENICAL SITUATIONS

Formal negotiations are not the context in which the problems most constantly face us. In joint Churches or congregations, and again on special ecumenical occasions in areas where congregations are still separate, there is often a desire to join together in communion *now*. This may be under the cover of no scheme at all, with no commitment to each other, and sometimes on opposite premisses as to the purpose and significance of intercommunion. We recognize that the instinct towards the practice (for instinct it is) is the outcome of a yearning, however inarticulate, for the oneness of God's people which is not only revealed in Scripture but, we may surmise, is also written deep in the heart of the Holy Spirit. We believe that the solution to these situations should not be a stretching or blurring of ecclesiological norms, but either an honest and agreed redrafting of them, or a frank admission of the fact that there are categories of departures from the norms which are held to be exceptions. In the latter case they must not call in question the norms nor disembowel them.

The "redrafting of norms" might well be possible in specified local areas. The obvious instance is the "area of ecumenical experiment". Here there will be actual plans and agreements (often of an irreversible kind) for local union. Anglican norms should meet such cases by becoming pluriform—i.e. a rewriting of ecclesiology may be desirable in local cases, though this should be sustained by a framework hammered out by the parent denominations setting limits to local rewriting. The aim at any rate must be to allow the practice of intercommunion to run alongside genuine ecumenical progress in different areas, and to do so for theologically respectable reasons. Our Group is hoping to return to this question.

This sort of situation seems to be touched on in *Intercommunion Today* in both paragraph 214(c), and paragraph 224(iv). We would offer two brief comments. First, as this is an ecclesiological question, it is unfortunate that it is listed in a series of exceptional cases in 214. Secondly 214(c) seems odd in that, although no reciprocity is in view, it refers itself to 188 which deals explicitly with reciprocal arrangements. 224(iv) is of course concerned with reciprocity, but here again ecclesiology is not very obvious. In this sphere we find the Bristol Commission better in its practice than its theology.

FURTHER CASES: (2) PASTORAL NEEDS

We said above that there were cases where we would desire not a redrafting of ecclesiology, but a simple admission of exceptions from the norms. These are the situations envisaged in the quotation earlier from our July Statement. They may vary from the case of a Presbyterian mother-in-law staying with an Anglican couple, or that of a Methodist scoutmaster attending the confirmation of boys from his troop, to the occasional ecumenical gatherings which are not yet provided with a clear ecclesiological framework. For these situations we have little new wisdom to offer. Like Vatican II we are concerned that behaviour which in practice seems out of accord with the formal demands of ideal ecclesiology should be allowable as an exception, but on the other hand *should be specifically prevented from calling the ideals in question*. The Commissions' recommendations seem to be sufficiently generously drawn to cover the right sort of cases. Our only request would therefore be that the relationship of such categories to a proper ecclesiology should be kept in view throughout. Under the limitations of space, against the shortage of time, and at an early stage of working together, we have not felt it possible to give detailed attention to relations with Churches beyond England. This would be crucial in a wide-ranging discussion of ecclesiology, but we judge it not the most urgent question in England in October 1969.

PROBLEMS IN HOSPITALITY

Most of the exceptional cases amount to an offering of hospitality, whereas the ecclesiologically based cases amount to sharing in what is in principle already common. If this distinction is clearly grasped, the problems in hospitality can be identified with some precision. The first problem is that the guest remains uncommitted to the fellowship in which he joins. This is no doubt right and proper for the merchant seaman ashore for a week-end in Buenos Aires or Archangel. But the privilege of communion is not only offered and commanded by Christ—it is also extended and administered by the particular Church. Just as the privilege demands a response when viewed in vertical terms, so it does when viewed in horizontal ones. If the sacrament is received lightly or thoughtlessly in this respect, it is being detached from its base in ecclesiology.

Perhaps the evangelical may be permitted to observe that this is a charge which might be brought against the Keswick (and Albert Hall) communions. They proclaim that they express oneness in Christ, but it is a special manifestation of the oneness of those who do not (and sometimes could not) live in an organic unity with each other for the rest of the year. Their categorization ought therefore to be "exceptional for conference pastoral reasons", which is a distinct departure from the advertised ecclesiological significance of "one in Christ".

The second problem is that the host congregation may offer the privilege of communion too lightly. On the one hand it is clear that Christians ought to be in communion with each other, etc., etc. But if the offer is made too lightly, the guest may not realize that in principle the sacrament demands response, and hosts may rob themselves of being able to bestow any particular privilege when true unity comes. It would be a disaster if a growing habit of intercommunion left the Churches with either no further desire for organic unity, or with a desire which had to admit that there would be no sacramental content to organic unity, which would be merely an administrative reshuffle. Each of these possible results would be the outcome of cutting loose sacramental practice from ecclesiology.

A third problem, which is actually often the *fons et origo* of the previous ones, is that many Christians view a sharing of communion as primarily an *experience*. This view apparently springs from a curious marriage between pietism and the *Zeitgeist*. Experience *per se* as the only criterion is autonomous and is self-justifying. If, however, it is as important to see the sharing of communion as a *significant act*, deriving its significance partly from its structural setting, then the act is *not* autonomous, but clearly dependent on other factors for its justification.

We say these things only as warnings. We gladly acknowledge that communion is a climax of worship, with individual as well as corporate implications. We also recognize at the same time that it not only expresses unity, but it also helps to create and sustain it (1 Cor. 10. 17). We are ready to be liberal as the Archbishops have said they wish to be. Only we hope that liberality can be defined not just in terms of stretching rules, but rather of acknowledging the exceptions from them that may be justified.

INTERCOMMUNION AND THE
ANGLICAN–METHODIST SCHEME

We may close with some animadversions on the relation of inter-communion with possible schemes for Anglican–Methodist unity. We honestly feel that the requirement of organic unity (the nebulous Stage Two of the recent Scheme) is paramount. That is why we have called in both our statements for a one-stage scheme which would focus the problems instead of dodging them. The circumstances in which intercommunion may be related in ec-clesiological terms to the movement towards such organic unity we have, we hope, set out clearly above. Our fear is that many of those who voted in favour of the recent Scheme ultimately wanted no more than intercommunion, though they would have had no particular objections to the long-term merging of the parallel episcopates. The actual commitment of Anglicans and Methodists to each other in (not intercommunion, but) communion pure and simple—this was not well brought into sight.

Thus our fear now is lest the growth of intercommunion (which in practice does not seem in the least hampered by the departure of the Scheme) become an end in itself, or at most an open-ended experiment. Its unguided growth could certainly rob any further consideration of the same Scheme of any sacramental significance whatsoever—making it more and more nakedly a power, politics, and prestige question. But it also lays upon critics of that Scheme the continuing duty to work unremittingly at the ecclesiological questions which both the Scheme and mere intercommunion seem to dodge. The task will not be to frustrate the practice of inter-communion, but to channel it in structured frameworks. To that task we continue to address ourselves.

COLIN BUCHANAN
✠ GRAHAM WILLESDEN

[*15 August 1969*]

Eucharistic Sacrifice—Some Interim Agreement

It is all too easy to make a man of straw, and then cheerfully burn him. This has been done by protagonists on both sides of the Catholic–Protestant divide, and the present writers confess that they have not been innocent of it. They have in fact been at logger-heads on this very subject in their published writings (see E. L. Mascall, *Corpus Christi* (2nd edn, p. 96) and Michael Green's paper "Christ's Sacrifice and Ours" in *Guidelines*, pp. 89–117). We mention this to show that we initially set out from deeply divergent approaches to the subject of eucharistic sacrifice and were by no means enamoured of easy solutions.

We are not so naive as to suppose that we have solved these problems, which have divided the best minds in Christendom for centuries. But mutual discussion and respect have shown that what unites us in our understanding of the Eucharist is far more significant than what divides us. It has shown that neither of us wishes to unchurch the other, nor to go our separate ways acting for all the world as if the other's viewpoint did not exist or was not to be taken seriously. We have no intention of smoothing over difficulties and brushing real problems under the carpet, though in common with many who have contributed to the growing *rapprochement* between Catholic and Protestant Christians during recent years we have found that many of our difficulties are not real. For instance, some Evangelicals need to be reminded that Catholics do not believe that they reimmolate Christ in the Eucharist or that the Eucharist is identical with his offering on the cross. Similarly, some Catholic churchmen will be relieved to hear that Evangelicals are not crypto-Zwinglians who regard the Holy Communion as a bare remembrance of a far-off event!

Our claim is a modest one. We hope that we have indicated ways in which two very different Christians from very different backgrounds can unite in saying many of the same things about this subject. Not all Anglo-Catholics and Evangelicals will be able to follow us in particular statements, perhaps, but it is our conviction that all ought to follow us in the determined attempt to understand Christians from a different tradition, respect them, and see how far we are, after all, seeking to say the same thing; where we are not, it may well be that our different emphases are trying to safeguard complementary aspects of Christian truth.

In the first place, we want to put it clearly on record that both our standpoints are rooted in Scripture. We are both shameless believers in such old-fashioned concepts as a transcendent Creator God who has revealed himself in history and supremely in the person of his Son. We believe in a real incarnation, a real atonement, an historic resurrection.

We also believe that man is made in the image of God and is called both to represent the Creator to the rest of the creation and to head up that creation's allegiance to the Creator. In this sense man might be called the priest of nature.

However, we recognize that sin has broken the proper relations between man and God. Man out of touch with God no longer mirrors accurately the Creator's glory to his creation, nor does he head up the creation's worship. We take very seriously the fallenness of man, and we are convinced that not only can he not save himself but that the only contribution he can make to his own redemption is the sin from which he needs to be redeemed. Both of the traditions we represent are, in their different ways, highly suspicious of that very British heresy, Pelagianism; both of us, in our different formulations of it, are determined to safeguard the crown rights of the Redeemer. We further agree that Christ is the Word made flesh (John 1. 14), the last Adam, whose achievement it is to be the true head of humanity in contrast to Adam's defection (Rom. 5. 12 ff; 1 Cor. 15. 21 ff). He brought restoration for ruin. He offered to the Father on the cross of Calvary "a full, perfect and sufficient sacrifice, oblation and satisfaction for the sins of the whole world", and, having entered into heaven in the strength of that sacrifice, he has an unchangeable priesthood (Heb. 7. 24 ff; 9. 24 ff). In him we have a High Priest who suits our need and is seated at the Father's right hand, his work of reconciliation completed, "for by a single offering he has perfected for all time those who are sanctified" (Heb. 10. 14; cf. Heb. 8. 1; Eph. 1. 20 ff).

It is not too much to stress, therefore, that, whereas the priests under the Levitical system were temporary, ineffectual, repetitive, and figurative, Jesus Christ (both Priest and Sacrifice in the New Covenant) is eternal, sufficient, unique, and real. His, in the last analysis, is the *only* priesthood and sacrifice; there is no other.

How, then, and in what respects, does the Church share in Christ's sacrifice? Is there a sense in which the Eucharist can be so described, by those who take the New Testament teaching as normative?

As we discussed these questions, we became more than ever aware of the semantic confusions which have bedevilled this controversy. Here are some instances:

The Evangelical does not naturally speak about *pleading* the sacrifice of Christ, because he knows it is already accepted by a God who needs no persuasion to be gracious. The Catholic does naturally use the term, but means by it that Christ's presence as the Lamb once slain in the midst of the throne is the silent plea for our acceptance. And with that sentiment his Evangelical friend can have no quarrel.

Similarly, Christ does not *present* his sacrifice, if by that is meant actively to offer to the Father the sacrifice of Calvary. He sits at the Father's side, his work of atonement accomplished (Heb. 7. 24) and by his living presence in heaven is the pledge of our acceptance: for "he ever lives to make intercession [*lit.* to be in the midst] for us" (Heb. 7. 25). Thus he may rightly be said to present his sacrifice, and so indeed may we, if by this we mean that man's hope of salvation is based squarely on that sacrifice once made and ever efficacious.

A further phrase which has caused great heartburnings is that of uniting our sufferings with those of Christ or joining our offerings to his. To the Evangelical this obscures the uniqueness of Jesus' achievement. His offering is perfect; ours is not. His suffering removed the sin of the world; ours does not. But the Catholic certainly does not wish to equate the Redeemer with the redeemed; in using this language he is giving expression to the New Testament truth that we can do nothing pleasing to God unless it is in Christ and with him. Of course, then, our offerings (imperfect as they are) and our sufferings (non-propitiatory as they are) must be joined with his. We are indeed partakers in Christ's sacrifice, but partakers in the benefits which flow from that sacrifice, not in the making of it. Nevertheless, Christians can make to God offerings which are acceptable in Christ. Man's original filial response, lost in Adam, is restored in Christ, in whom we are incorporate (Gal. 4. 1 ff; cf. Rom. 8. 17; 1 Cor. 12. 12 ff). There is nothing improper in the idea of our offering to God, even though all we have comes from him in the first place, just as there is nothing improper (but, rather, delightful) in the gift of a child to his father out of money the father has given him.

This leads us to another deep-seated confusion, which, as before, is basically due to the ambiguities of language. Both Catholic and Evangelical want to do justice to the once-for-allness of the atonement and to the ongoing grace of God in the soul of man. We have traditionally done it by making opposite claims. The Evangelical has stoutly asserted that the Eucharist is not a sacrifice (or, at most, a responsive one), in order to safeguard the uniqueness of Calvary; the Catholic has asserted that the Eucharist is a sacrifice because it is integrally related to the sacrifice *par excellence*, the only sacrifice a Christian knows, namely that same cross and resurrection in all its uniqueness. It is a curious fact that both sides have tended to suspect the other of Pelagianism. The Evangelical has a shrewd suspicion that the Catholic has never understood the once-for-allness of the atonement and justification and is, therefore, always anxious to be making a sacrifice, and, because God is obviously satisfied with no other sacrifice than that of his Son, Catholics must needs try to offer that; does that not sniff of a doctrine of "works"? The Catholic, on the other hand, has no liking for his Evangelical brother's reiteration of the distinction between "sacrifices propitiatory" and "other sacrifices" (to use Cranmer's celebrated disjunction), for, when the Protestant asserts that the only sacrifice at the Eucharist is one of praise and thanksgiving, in response to Christ's once-for-all sacrifice for us, this merely seems as if he for his part is determined to offer God something that is different from the sacrifice of Christ! We have both found it helpful to recall afresh that any genuine Christian understanding of the meaning of sacrifice must derive from what Jesus crucified and risen did for sinful men; and that any sense in which we use the word for Christian worship or service, praise or self-dedication, must be derived but not isolated from that supreme paradigm of sacrifice.

It is probably an indication of the failure of most of Christendom to grasp both in experience and doctrine the truth of the resurrection, that both sides in this controversy suspect the other of undue emphasis on the *death* of Christ. The Catholic cannot understand why the Evangelical is so determined to equate sacrifice with death, as though a dead Christ was what he was determined at all costs to have. The Evangelical views with disquiet Catholic preoccupation with offering the sacrifice of Christ and speculation about some supposed self-immolation of Christ at the heavenly altar. Both positions are right in stressing the necessary link between Christ's sin-offering and death. Both are liable to misunderstanding if the radiance of the risen Lord does not shine out through their worship.

The New Testament does not call the Eucharist a sacrifice, nor does it call its ministers sacrificing priests (*hiereis*), although there was every inducement both from Old Testament precedent and from pagan parallels to do so. The Epistle to the Hebrews might have made enormous play with both concepts, but significantly did not. We take this reserve on the part of the earliest Christians very seriously as a warning against the misunderstandings which can creep into the understanding of the Eucharist once sacrificial terminology is used.

However, it seems to us that if a Christian's prayer, evangelism, almsgiving, and self-dedication can be called a sacrifice, as they are so called in the New Testament (Rom. 12. 1; Phil. 2. 17; 4. 18; Heb. 13. 15–16; 1 Pet. 2. 5), it is a legitimate term for the Eucharist, which is the supreme meeting-place of Christ and his people, the supreme emblem both of his grace and our response. The Eucharist, by Christ's own "institution and promise" (Article 26), is integrally related to his sacrifice for us upon the cross; it is a sacrament of our redemption by Christ's death. It is therefore natural enough to apply to the sign the term appropriate to the thing signified; accordingly, there is even good sense in calling baptism a sacrifice, as George Every has shown in his book *The Baptismal Sacrifice*, because baptism no less than the Eucharist is grounded in the sacrifice of Christ. It was in this sense that the Passover was sometimes called a sacrifice in Israel. Both Eucharist and Passover, though not themselves expiatory sacrifices, nonetheless commemorate one and do so by divine appointment. Moreover, expiation apart, there is a further sense in which the Eucharist is a sacrifice. It is a counterpart both to the peace-offering and to the burnt-offering sacrifices of the Old Covenant. Like the former, it is a feast shared with the Lord. Like the latter, it is a pledge of our total devotion to the one who gave himself for us. And it was in this sense that the early Church began to speak of the Eucharist as a sacrifice. From the days of the Didache (at the end of the first century) onwards the Holy Communion was seen as the fulfilment of Malachi 1. 11, that a pure offering would be offered in every place among the Gentiles. Justin carefully explains to us what is meant. He tells us that, just as the leper, cleansed from his disease, offered the cereal offering (to which Malachi alludes) as a sacrifice of thanksgiving and devotion to God, so the Christian, cleansed from the defilement of his sin, offers the bread of the Eucharist as a thanksgiving to God for his creative and redemptive work (*Dialogue* 41).

Sacrifice means offering. What, then, do we offer at the Eucharist? Christ offered himself on the cross in our stead and without our aid, and we certainly cannot repeat that offering. We do, on the other hand, offer (to quote from ch. 3 above) "not merely 'the fruit of our lips'; not merely undefined 'spiritual sacrifices'; not merely ourselves, considered apart from Christ; not even ourselves in Christ, if that is seen in separation from our feeding on Christ; but ourselves as reappropriated by Christ".[1] The sacrament which communicates to us afresh the benefits of Christ's passion communicates to us no less immediately and certainly, both as redeemed individuals and as members of his redeemed body the Church, the demands which his passion makes upon us. And thus we are delivered from a purely individualistic understanding. We who offer ourselves by communicating have died and risen with Christ in our baptism (Rom. 6. 1 ff); and "we, though many, are one body in Christ, and individually members one of another" (Rom. 12. 5; cf. 1 Cor. 10. 15 ff; Eph. 5. 30). Therefore, in drinking from the one cup and eating the one bread of the Eucharist, we have *koinonia* (communion, participation) in the sacrificial blood of Christ and in his body. We are thus simultaneously the beneficiaries, communicating in his body given on the cross, and participating members of his body which is the Church (cf. 1 Cor. 10. 14–17, where both concepts of "body" are put in juxtaposition, as we have done here, in a eucharistic context). In the act of communicating, the Church, reintegrated and reappropriated by the one means of grace, is made a living sacrifice to God.

---

[1] See ch. 3, p. 59 above.

If these are the factors involved in the desire of many churchmen to call the Eucharist a sacrifice, then, so long as there is no suggestion that the sacrifice of the Eucharist supplements or repeats the once-for-all offering on Calvary, and so long as the distinction between the Saviour and the saved is scrupulously safeguarded, Evangelicals and Catholics can say Amen.

MICHAEL GREEN

E. L. MASCALL

8 January 1970

BIBLIOGRAPHY ON EUCHARISTIC SACRIFICE

MICHAEL GREEN

Essay "Eucharistic Sacrifice in the New Testament and the Early Fathers" in *Eucharistic Sacrifice*, ed. J. I. Packer. Church Book Room Press 1962.

Called to Serve (ch. 7). Hodder and Stoughton 1964.

Essay "Christ's Sacrifice and Ours" in *Guidelines*, ed. J. I. Packer. Falcon Books 1967.

Article "Christ's Sacrifice and Ours" in *One in Christ* (Vol. IV, no. 3, 1968).

E. L. MASCALL

Corpus Christi: Essays on the Church and Eucharist. Longmans, 2nd edn 1965.

Articles "Eucharistic Doctrine after Vatican II" in *Church Quarterly Review* (January and April 1968).

Other members of the team:

COLIN BUCHANAN

The New Communion Service—Reasons for Dissent. Church Book Room Press 1966 (reprinted as article in *The Churchman*, Summer 1966).

Joint Article (with R. T. Beckwith) "'This Bread and this Cup': An Evangelical Rejoinder" in *Theology* (June 1967).

Editor *Modern Anglican Liturgies* (ch. 2). Oxford University Press 1968.

J. I. PACKER

Editor of *Eucharistic Sacrifice*, Church Book Room Press 1962, and essay in this "Introduction: Lambeth 1958".

A Bog of Illogic
or The Service of Reconciliation
and the Law of Non-Contradiction

The aim of this book has been positive—to indicate a way forward from the existing ecumenical log-jam. Nevertheless it is abundantly clear that at the time of writing some at least of the Anglican and Methodist leadership considers that the only log-jam is a synodical one, that out of sheer perverseness a small unrepresentative minority has blocked what the two Churches demonstrably wanted, and has blocked it irrespective of its merits. For our part we are convinced that the log-jam exists irremovably in the actual contents of the Scheme on which we so recently voted, and that no amount of screwing up the support of the members of Convocation or the General Synod to some magic figure like 75% would alter that fact. There are several features of this log-jam (e.g. the two-stage concept) which we have discussed earlier. But the key to it is the Service of Reconciliation, and no amount of presenting alternative ways forward can ever win support until and unless this hard objective fact is grasped. To that extent we are under compulsion to expose the inner contradictions of the Service; to that extent we have to look backward at this point.

The features of the Service we propose to examine are explicit in the liturgical text or the constitutional setting proposed for it in the two Churches. We do not here, therefore, dilate upon the question of opposite intentions in the various participants, nor upon the mutually exclusive rationales of it presented to the Anglican Convocations and the Methodist Conference. These *prima facie* breaches of the law of non-contradiction are potentially exceedingly serious, but they lie outside our brief.

Before analysing the Service it is well to recall a big presupposition of the rite—the concept that once a man is ordained he is ordained within that order for life. Virtually all Churches, Roman, Eastern, Anglican, and non-episcopalian alike, function on this theory. We discuss it briefly in ch. 4 above. The relevance to the present issue does not lie in its viability or non-viability as a theological concept; it lies simply in its being assumed in the Churches. It is *the* great presupposition to the Service of Reconciliation.[1]

This said, it remains to list out the illogic of the rite under twelve separate heads:

I. WHERE HAVE THE FOUNDATIONS GONE?

Scripture records a man who built his house upon the sand. The removal of the foundations of his house led inevitably to the building's collapse. Or was it inevitable? Perhaps the man could have learned from the architects of the rite under review. They built on sand, watched the sand wash away in the storm, and, behold, their house still stood. This process can be traced from its beginning in 1958. Then the *Interim Statement* rejected anything like a C.S.I. method of bringing together ministries on the grounds that, until the original ministers had died off, "meanwhile within the Methodist Church there would be two classes of ministers" (p. 40). This fact being fatal to the C.S.I. method the Conversationalists turned to "a bolder and richer possibility"—"*the unification of both ministries at the start*". On this foundation they built—on the solid ground that all ministers of both Churches would be "unified" on a common roll, with common orders and common standing in both Churches. The solid ground proved in the event to be nothing but sand. Once the Methodist Conference in 1965 had built into the Unity Commission's terms of reference the task of "Consideration of the position of any clergy and ministers who cannot, in good conscience, take part in the Service of Reconciliation, so as to safeguard their status...",[2] the sand was starting to wash away. This might have been simply a theoretical consideration; but it was taken seriously by the Unity Commission, who provided most charitably for such men,[3] and thereby *aided the washing away of the*

---

[1] It *might* in principle be open to theological dispute. Any rationale of the Service, which ends up by saying "well, what does it matter if people *are* ordained twice?", ought at the same time to lay out the ground on which the traditional "once-for-life" view of ordination can be questioned. This has simply not been done, and without it no rationale leading to this question can be accepted as plausible. The more obvious and frequent solution to the riddle of the Service is that it is assimilating its participants into the traditional "once-for-life" pattern. The "once-for-life" pattern itself we have expounded above in ch. 4, pp. 83–4 above.

[2] *Towards Reconciliation*, p. 78; *The Scheme*, p. 180.

[3] *The Scheme*, paras. 167–72, pp. 55–7.

foundation. Finally, although the Methodist Conference did not devise any way of discovering what proportion of Methodist ministers would receive the laying on of hands in the Service, the Church of England held a straw vote (a much better description of it than a referendum) and found that 5621 beneficed or licensed clergy (out of a voting total of 16,376) declared they would not attend. The sandy foundation was now fully departed, but, marvel of marvels, 69% of the Convocation and 77% of the Methodist Conference were prepared to vote that the building would stand without the foundations.[1] Possibly they thought that their votes would do as alternative foundations. Or had they forgotten that they needed foundations for the Service on which they hoped to build two more stages at least?

2. UNIFYING BY DIVIDING

It may be as well to spell out the actual classes of ministers which the unification rite (so piously avoiding the "two classes" of C.S.I.) bid fair to create. These were as follows:

(a) *Anglicans refusing full communion to Methodists.* Many of the 5621 mentioned above took the view that episcopal ordination was necessary for full communion, and was not in fact going to be conferred in the Service of Reconciliation. These men, whilst resting on their own episcopal ordination and refusing to participate in the Service, seemed likely to become what the editor of *Theology* (October 1969) called "a new collection of non-jurors".

(b) *Anglicans granting full communion to Methodists without themselves attending the Service.* The evangelical inquiry, based on the Open Letter signed by fifty-two Evangelicals in summer 1968, found just over 1000 clergy who said they would form this class. This class, whilst not non-juring, would not have been on the common roll of the unified, and their position would have been highly anomalous.

(c) *Anglicans who received the laying on of hands in the Service.* For these purposes, which are purely outward ones, these men constitute a single group—the largest single group in either Church.

[1] The figures are set out in Appendix 6, pp. 208–11.

(*d*) *Anglicans ordained after the inauguration of Stage One.* Whereas the class (*c*) above would be reckoned as acceptable to the Methodists because they had *both* episcopal ordination *and* Methodist unification, this class would be acceptable solely on the grounds of episcopal ordination. It is unclear whether this straight acceptability would have been built upon the supposed "reconciliation" of the two Churches, or upon the "reconciled" status of the ordaining bishop. If the former, then it would be arguable that the reconciliation of Churches logically entails the reconciliation of ministers, and the act of ministerial reconciliation is strictly redundant and misleading. If the latter, then the question arises as to the potential status of a minister ordained by one of the two diocesans who said they themselves would not participate in the Service. Were they due to go on providing quasi-non-juring ministers for the Church for many years ahead? Or would their newly ordained presbyters have had to betake themselves to some local Methodist bishop in order to get this Methodist pedigree into their family tree of orders? It seems hard on an ordinand that by sheer freak of the geography of where he would serve his title he might have found himself ordained as "unreconciled"!

(*e*) *Methodists who received the laying on of hands in the Service.* This is the key class. These are the men who were promised full acceptability in the Church of England by the Draft Bill.[1] Yet, as it is probable that their orders would still not have been recognized by those in class (*a*) above, it is clear that the Draft Bill purported to promise what could not be attained.

(*f*) *Methodists who did not receive the laying on of hands in the Service.* These men were those who were likely to suffer most under the Scheme's provisions, and they would have been under great pressure to leave Methodism. Where they remained, they would have been officially unacceptable to the Church of England (as having no suggestion even of episcopal ordination in their pedigree), though they might have been treated as equal to class (*e*) ministers by Anglicans in class (*b*). Their sole comfort (having been omitted from the interchangeability provisions of the Draft Bill) lay in the promise of para. 169 that no official list would differentiate between them and classes (*e*) and (*g*). This minute gain on the swings, however, had an equal and opposite loss on the round-

---

[1] *The Scheme*, pp. 103–9, paras. 320–9.

abouts. The "no listing" provision, if it had been operated, would have made not only class (a), but also quite a proportion of class (b) even, suspicious as to the credentials of *all* Methodist ministers. The other possibility was that the "no listing" would not have been operated, and that these ministers would have been ecclesiastical lepers for the rest of their days.[1]

(g) *Methodists ordained after the inauguration of Stage One.* These men ought in principle to have had orders acceptable to all other classes. The only faint query which would have hung round them would have been a refusal by a small number of those in class (a) to recognize the Methodist episcopate as standing in the historic episcopate (through lack of clear intention), and thus even this class would not have stood totally on a par with (c) and (d).

3. HALF-FULL FULL COMMUNION

"Full communion" has for at least a decade clearly meant the full interchangeability of all ministers of two Churches. The seven classes listed out above show how vain a dream this would have been for the contemplated Stage One. Yet no one gave official recognition to the fact. Stage One remained the era of "full communion". The very Draft Bill simultaneously uses this term "full communion" (in the preamble and in para. 3(1)) and excludes the "unreconciled" from its provisions. This arises from the Methodist terms of reference for the Unity Commission (partly quoted above), which provide not only that their ministers may stay away, but also that this may happen "without jeopardizing the attainment of full communion between the two Churches". As long as episcopal ordination (or even a semblance of it) is required by the Church of England for ministers to be acceptable, this Methodist proviso in the terms of reference could not be fulfilled. The Commission could have admitted this and come to one of the following recommendations:

Either (a) To change the Church of England's rules so that Methodist (non-episcopal) ordination would be acceptable in the Church of England. This would have made the Service of Reconciliation completely redundant.

---

[1] It is not difficult to imagine their being required to exhibit notices saying, "Warning to Anglican communicants—'unreconciled' minister"!

Or (b) To acknowledge that full communion was unattainable.

Or (c) To refuse to make provision for non-participants in the Service of Reconciliation (in accordance with the original rationale).

What the Commission actually did was to go covertly for (*b*), but to cover up its violating of the impossible terms of reference by *calling* the resultant relationship between the two Churches "full communion" by a linguistic deviousness pioneered by Humpty-Dumpty.[1]

4. ONCE-FOR-ALL—FREQUENTLY

The whole history of the Service since 1963 has seen a havering between the concept that two Churches were being reconciled to each other, and the concept that a series of individual ministers were being reconciled to each other as individuals. Eric Kemp's account[2] of the changes made from 1967 to 1968 shows that the Commission felt this tension and tried to move somewhat nearer to the corporate concept in the final report. However, the truth was and is impossible to conceal: that the aim was to bring all ministers (especially Methodist ministers) individually "under the yoke", and that no emphasis on the corporate in terms of verbal titivation should frustrate the necessary treatment of each minister individually. Much of the public propaganda for the Scheme in fact treated the Service as a once-for-all corporate reconciliation which, having once occurred, would then cease forever, whilst the Ordinal held pride of place as the lasting document to straightening out the ministry.

But to cease forever was impossible for the Service. What about those in hospital or abroad on holiday? Or those who refused to go, but later changed their minds? Or those who had been ordained elsewhere and later come to England? Or those who had gone from England to serve the overseas Church and did not return till, say, 1985? It was insufficient that they should take their place in the

---

[1] It does use "full communion" in its accepted sense in paras. 153 ff to describe relations with *other* Churches, and thus confesses in para. 167 that, when it says "full communion" about this relationship, it does not really mean it.

[2] *The Anglican–Methodist Unity Scheme* by E. W. Kemp and F. Colquhoun, circulated free to all incumbents in May 1969 (labelled 2*s*. 6*d*., no publisher indicated, but printed in Windsor).

ranks of the ministry of the (corporately) reconciled Churches. They would need the treatment individually. And although the Church of England might well have been tempted on the eve of the 1978 Lambeth Conference (if such should ever be) to spare the near-1000 bishops from overseas a visit to Westminster Central Hall to have Methodist episcopal hands laid on them to make them acceptable to minister in the Church of England [sic!]—yet, if Methodists coming home from overseas were to have such treatment, the Church of England would either have to insist that her visitors submitted to it, or would have to admit that the mutuality in the laying on of hands was a fiction. If Methodists from overseas did not have such treatment, then the "unreconciled" element (class (f) above) might persist for generations ahead. In fact the Draft Bill (para. 326) carefully provides for this possibility by allowing the repetition of the Service. But this, it must be pointed out, explodes the once-for-all corporate reconciliation rationale; it is a naked catching up on errant individuals. It may be most aptly characterized as "Bishops at the Customs".

5. A CORPORATE RELATIONSHIP—INDIVIDUALLY

If we add the two previous points together, we come to a very curious conclusion. "Full communion" in the Commission's new sense has no corporate reference. It has nothing to do with relations between Churches. It does not imply the acceptance by one Church of the ministry of the other. It simply means the acceptance by individual ministers of one Church of individual ministers of the other. This fact is neatly attested by a statement by the Bishop of London: "If he [an unreconciled minister] does not wish to enter personally into full communion with the Methodist Church he cannot be compelled to do so."[1] The idea of individuals going into "full communion" with anybody is grotesque. Yet the term had so much changed its meaning on the Unity Commission that the Bishop found it natural to give it its new sense when speaking in public. The astonishing thing is that he does not seem to have been taken up on it. On this basis no Church would know whether it was in full communion with another until it had carried out an exhaustive inquiry into the attitude of every single minister individually to see whether each would personally act on the provisions.

[1] *Anglican–Methodist Conversations* (C.I.O. 1967), p. 7.

It would be interesting to see the effect of this inquiry in relation to, say, our "full communion" with the Old Catholics (and we might expect their response to the suggestion of an inquiry to be pretty apoplectic). This feature of the recent Scheme is not far from a proposal to suspend the proposition "all sheep are animals" upon an investigation of every single sheep to see its characteristics. The truth is that "full communion" (in its usual meaning) involves a potential, not an actual, practice, and can therefore be determined corporately.

6. THE LAW OF DIMINISHING RETURNS

If the only viable way to tie the Methodist ministry into the historic episcopate is to have a mutual laying on of hands throughout the ministry of both Churches, how would the ministers of the future Congregationalist–Presbyterian Church ever be tied to the resultant ministry? The answer must be either this way also or another way. If there is another way, then, to put it mildly, we ought to be allowed to inspect it to see whether it would be viable for integrating the Methodist ministry also. If there is no other way, we must face the logic of the course on which the Service of Reconciliation is setting us. There may be some outward plausibility in having a mutuality between 18,000 clergy and 3500 (or whatever the respective numbers are). The resultant 21,500 will then have to go through the same process again *vis-à-vis* the, say, 1500 ministers of the Congregational–Presbyterian Church. The resultant 23,000 ministers will still not have "arrived" at fully integrated ecumenical orders. Smaller denominations will yet emerge to cast their ministerial widow's mite into the treasury of the Service of Reconciliation along with our much-integrated riches. Suppose we end up with 25 ministers of the Countess of Huntingdon's Connexion laying their hands upon 23,000 ministers or more of a united Church of this land. Can the laying-on of hands really prove more than a rather bad cartoon joke in such a case? Or have we really all got to express our penitence for the sins of the past, our need of grace for reconciliation through the laying on of their hands, our agnosticism about what God is thereby doing, in a service attended by ministers of two Churches in the proportions of rather over 700 to 1? When does liturgy of this sort shed its solemnity and become just an expensive giggle?

Yet the logical defect of the Service is not simply the numerical disparity involved—though it is arguable that the sheer Anglican-Methodist disparity would itself make an actual performance of the rite look oddly lopsided. The defect lies in the necessity for seeming to assert some lack in orders which no one has previously queried. The step of humility which leads to the spoof mutuality in the Service of Reconciliation leads logically on to a further step of humility for all who have been through the first round of the Service's administration. If we add together the possible future false humilities to which we might be committing ourselves as we embark on this course, it is quite probable that we have nothing clear we can assert about our orders now at all.

A prophet might prefer the other horn of the dilemma. We are *bound* to come one day to some other method of integration. If we cannot continue this method, we are bound to repent of it. It is exactly the problem a finance minister will face who solves his troubles by inflation. He will quickly have to ask himself whether he wishes to continue a remedy which is worse than the disease it cures, or whether he will manfully repent of it. Those who discern that he will face this choice one day cannot be accused of political cynicism or opportunism if they decline to go with him on his first slippery downwards step.

7. CANONICAL BUT EMBARGOED

We now turn to the meaning the Service has in terms of the status of Methodist participants. The Draft Bill sedulously avoids an un-packing of the Service's meaning—it merely permits the Methodist recipients to minister in the Church of England on the same terms as those who have been explicitly episcopally ordained. However, the Draft Bill is not the only interpretative document in the field. The 1969 Canon B 12 (para. 1) reads: "No person shall consecrate and administer the holy sacrament of the Lord's Supper unless he shall have been ordained priest by episcopal ordination in accordance with the provisions of Canon C 1." This Canon was, remarkably in point of time, promulged at the May 1969 joint session of the Canterbury and York Convocations which came within a whisker of giving the Service of Reconciliation 75 % approval.[1] Here there is no exception, no alternative. Even if, which we would be prepared

---

[1] See the figures on p. 210.

to dispute, Canon C1 can include a reference to the Service of Reconciliation,[1] yet B12 says that this must make the man a "priest by episcopal ordination". Thus this Canon sits over the Service of Reconciliation as the Church of England's infallible interpreter of the rite. The dilemma here is that *either* the Methodist minister has now been episcopally ordained *or* he is ineligible to consecrate the sacrament in the Church of England.

All this might in theory be perfectly acceptable, but it clashes with the official rationale of the Service. We therefore seemed to be heading for a situation whereby every Anglican was prohibited in the Service from saying what was happening, but would triumphantly (or perhaps penitently) point out to his Methodist friends afterwards what had in fact happened. The meaning of the Service was indeed canonical but embargoed.

8. THE MAGNIFICENT DOUBLE-THINK

Did this mean that the Methodist minister was not allowed to think he had not been ordained (as he has been solemnly assured by Dr Harold Roberts that he would be able to think—indeed as Dr Roberts has frequently asserted would be objectively the case)? Well, he would not need to think he had been episcopally ordained so long as he remained in Methodism. But the moment he wished to celebrate communion in the Church of England Canon B12 would have got him. If a bishop asked for a clear undertaking from his clergy that Canon B12 would be observed, the only acceptable guest celebrants would be episcopally ordained ones. And if a Methodist minister were examined as to whether he fulfilled the requirements, he would either have to say "yes" or "no". The dilemma here is most painful. The only useful solution would be to answer "yes" when needing to celebrate in the Church of England, but "no" on return to his Methodist situation. This is a double-think approaching the heroic.

---

[1] The crucial words in C1 are "the Ordinal or any form of service alternative thereto". But the Anglican understanding of "alternative services" must make this mean "another Ordinal". So any concealed reference to the Service can only be referring to it as an Ordinal.

9. DEFINED AGNOSTICISM AND UNDEFINED CERTAINTY

This point can be made in a nutshell. How is it that we cannot know what God wants to do (in response to our indefinite prayers), but we can know that what *he* wants *us* to do is to lay hands on each other as the core of the rite (whilst we can negotiate about the sort of words which will enable us to remain agnostic and God to be fully active)? Or could it be that, when the smokescreen is blown away, the only thing he or we can be interested in is getting Methodists episcopally ordained without saying so in so many words? The "canonical but embargoed" interpretation is the foundation-principle of the liturgical edifice.

10. SPOOF MUTUALITY

The cumulative impact of the previous points is enough to make us ask seriously what is supposed to be happening when Methodists lay hands on Anglicans. The answer is bound to boil down to the dilemma that there must be a defect in either the Anglican orders or the Anglican jurisdiction. But no Methodist or Anglican believes the former, and no Anglican or Methodist would attempt to correct the latter by the laying on of hands. So where are we? Or could we have so rationalized the proceeding that we actually think our ministers will have special resources of grace ministered to them this way that will be available no other way? If so, of course, then the more frequently the better. But do we believe that? And if we do, why do we not do it with Old Catholics, or with ex-Roman Catholics, or in any other situation where full communion or recognition of orders may lead to demanding ministerial tasks for which great grace is needed?

11. SAUCE FOR THE GOOSE

Half the answer to the rhetorical question above is easy to supply. "Soon we would have been doing." The requirements of spoof mutuality would lay their dead hands on all movements of ministers into both the two Churches. Methodists from elsewhere would have to receive the rite at the customs—yes, and so therefore would the Anglicans. If Methodists need this rite, all must have it—and the all includes Roman Catholic and Eastern Orthodox priests as well as American pisky bishops at Lambeth 1978. The two Churches thus break down a barrier between themselves by erecting another one round themselves against the rest of Christendom. They practise "full communion" (*exceptis excipiendis!*) with each other by withdrawing recognition from all other orders in the world. They make the only recognizable bases for ministry episcopal ordination in their two Churches *after* inauguration, or participation in a Service of Reconciliation—ordination before the Service or outside the two Churches is simply irrelevant. If some ministers are tolerated without these qualifications, they are recognizably second-class. It might not have been long before Rome recognized our orders as primitive and genuine from her standpoint, but we had withdrawn recognition from her as insufficiently latter-day and as lacking Methodist integration from our standpoint. Possibly this Appendix could have been refurbished as an ace to trump *Apostolicae curae.*

12. CATHOLIC BUT NOT UNIVERSAL

The upshot of the argument above is that every national or other sort of united Church which practised a Service of Reconciliation type of ministerial integration would set up its own distinctive orders behind the new barrier it had erected round its participating Churches. The rite itself must (for the first time in the Anglican tradition) specify a particular Church within which the orders are conferred,[1] and, although this is not true of the Ordinal, it has already been made clear that the assumption must be that the Ordinal is sufficient only if the ordaining bishop has the Unifical [*sic?*—or Reconcilial?] somewhere in his pedigree. It would be difficult, even heroic again, to keep records of whether episcopally ordained ministers had "English-Reconciled" orders or not, but, if Crockford's were forbidden to do the listing, the job would still have to be done. It might be in records kept by the bishops-at-the-customs or it might be in the neatly domesticated letters of catholic orders issued to each minister.

The situation to which we would then be approaching is one in which every country with such a rite would have its own indigenized and customs-protected brand of orders. The qualifications to

---

[1] This is explicit at several points in the text of the Service, including the prayer before the laying on of hands and the welcoming formula after it.

minister in one Church would be simply irrelevant in another. Each Church would pretentiously insist that its orders must now be recognizable by others, whilst each in turn systematically withdrew recognition from all others. The more united Churches there came to be, the worse would be the confusion.

It will be helpful to recall the *fons et origo* of this. The rite is designed to include the laying on of a bishop's hands on those who have never had it before. We have shown above that it is in such cases a covertly designed episcopal ordination. It is intended to bring the recipient into the historic succession which is part of the understanding of "catholic" orders.[1] Yet the root meaning of "catholic" is "universal", and at this point the Service severs every participant, whatever his background of orders, from others in the same succession. Thus historic succession is established at the expense of true catholicity. It would be well in such Churches to drop the term "catholic" altogether. Their link with "catholic" orders would be purely a pedigree traceable in chronology back to the first Service of Reconciliation and the participation in it of bishops in the historic succession. But it would only be by naked pedigree that the link with "catholic" orders would be maintained —a situation exactly comparable to that of the lines of succession derived from *episcopi vagantes*. Once again the remedy is worse than the disease.

The above list of twelve illogicalities makes no pretence to exhaustiveness.[2] But it is sufficient to set up a *prima facie* claim that the Service of Reconciliation defies the law of non-contradiction in itself and in its context. If this is so, it would be less than honest to avoid pointing out the implications for some of the ministerial integration rites on the same lines elsewhere. It is our expectation that the first country to form a united Church on this basis will produce such ecumenical confusion that it will also be the last. Our fear is lest North India be the guinea-pig in this doomed experiment, but it probably *had* to be somewhere. The Christian

---

[1] The resolution before the Convocations in May 1969 spoke of "the continuance of Catholic orders" about the Ordinal, and "theologically adequate to make the two ministries mutually acceptable" about the Service of Reconciliation—see p. 210.

[2] This treatment omits the apparent illogicality of insisting on a Service of Reconciliation at Stage One, whilst seeming to promise a South India solution at Stage Two. It is like asserting one is catching a train for Scotland from Victoria or Charing Cross—the assertion is audible but the place of departure cannot lead to the asserted destination.

Church at large seems incapable of foreseeing the confusion, so it is inevitable that some Church should actually make the mistake so that others can learn from it. If they do, the inaugurators may be able to take retrospective action to salvage their own ministerial regulations from chaos. We say this not to dissuade the North Indians (for they must act in accordance with their own consciences not ours), but to set their action on a world scene. Their one-stage scheme, whilst avoiding some of the pitfalls of our English two-stage one, still has a unification Service open to several of the charges above. This can best be drawn out by imagining that the Nigerians[1] had been able to go ahead in December 1965 and asking ourselves what would have occurred.

The Nigerians had no desire to impart episcopal ordination in their unifical. They therefore had a laying on of a bishop's hands on non-episcopal ministers (among others) but no clear statement as to its purpose. Their procedure (as the North Indian one now is) was to go ahead first and ask the Church of England for full communion after. The Convocations would then have been asked for a vote on whether or not to go into full communion with Nigeria. But the presupposition in the Convocation debate would necessarily have been the invariable requirement by the Church of England of episcopal ordination for those who minister in it. It is unthinkable that the Act of Uniformity, the Preface to the 1662 Ordinal, and the (then draft) Canon B12 would have been overthrown or rewritten for the sake of the united Church of Nigeria. Thus, if full communion had been granted, it would have been on the understanding that the unifical had provided episcopal ordination. This in turn might well have led to the sort of interrogation anticipated above on p. 202 in which a "unified" Nigerian minister had to state whether or not he had been episcopally ordained. And once he did that the fat would have been in the fire.

At the same time the "full communion" would have been unilateral. Anglican and Methodist ministers from England would alike have been met by a Nigerian bishop at the customs and "unified" with the rite which virtually disregarded their previous

---

[1] We cite the Nigerians, whose scheme was due for consummation in December 1965, not in order to applaud the collapse of that scheme—a collapse which caused widespread grief. It is simply that, if the scheme had been implemented, the Nigerians would have been the first Christians in the world to use this "laying-on-of-hands-all-round" recipe. Thus they would have been a test case, and it is as a hypothetical test case we cite them.

ordination but made them acceptable together to minister in the Nigerian Church. "Full communion" would have become a fading term, only really applicable to old-fashioned denominations which had not yet been involved in unification rites. If the Church of England had denied full communion to South India,[1] the Nigerian Church, her elbow twisted by the Lambeth Conference of 1958 and the Lambeth Consultative Committee thereafter, would deny full communion to the Church of England—and the Church of England's only escape from this would be to launch her own Service of Reconciliation and deny full communion back to the Nigerians. If the world Church is becoming a global village, yet the inhabitants are still busily raising the barriers higher between their respective dwellings.

[1] If of course the 1968 Lambeth resolutions urging full communion with South India had in time been acted on, the reverse would have happened. Then the Nigerians would have undergone a totally redundant rite for the sake of a benefit they would have received in any case. This may yet prove true in North India and elsewhere. And the fact that the rite is redundant will not necessarily reduce its own exclusive implications.

The Anglican–Methodist Voting Statistics: a Summary of the Voting in both Churches in 1968–9

THE CHURCH OF ENGLAND

(a) Diocesan Conference Voting in Total (November 1968 to January 1969)

	Clergy			Laity		
	Yes	No	No vote	Yes	No	No vote
1. Does the Conference agree that unity should be sought in two stages, namely the establishment of full communion followed later by the union of the two Churches?[1]	8477	2329	395	10,244	1799	331
2. Does the Conference approve the proposed Ordinal?	8560	1985	631	8947	1997	1362
3. Does the Conference approve the proposed Service of Reconciliation?	6441	4216	512	7735	3306	1244
4. Does the Conference wish the Convocations to give final approval to the inauguration of Stage One?	7087	3548	425	8986	2784	548

[1] The dioceses did not originally know whether question 1 referred to the basic principle of a two-stage scheme, or the particular two-stage scheme under discussion. The Archbishop of Canterbury circularized diocesan bishops in December 1968 to notify them that it referred to the basic principle only, but several Conferences had by then voted. Later the House of Laity conducted its debate on the opposite presupposition and voted accordingly.

(b) The House of Laity of the Church Assembly (14 February and 7 June 1969)

	For	Against	Abstentions
1. This House agrees that unity with the Methodist Church should be sought in two stages, namely the establishment of full communion followed later by the union of the Churches. (14 Feb.)	104	81	1
2. This House generally approves the proposed Ordinal. (14 Feb.)	144	25	11
3. This House generally approves the proposed Service of Reconciliation. (7 June)	109	96	3
4. This House desires that the Convocations should give final approval to the inauguration of Stage One of the proposals for unity with the Methodist Church. (7 June)	115	105	1

The House of Laity was the only body to pass other resolutions on the subject (apart from one or two diocesan conferences). After the vote on the fourth resolution above they passed another motion in three parts as follows:

	For	Against	Abstentions
(a) This House strongly affirms its desire for organic unity with the Methodist Church and also with other Churches with whom agreement can be reached.	Nem. Con.		—
(b) This House recognizes that the present unity scheme is likely to lead to divisions within both the Methodist and Anglican Churches.	124	73	16
(c) This House requests the Convocations to arrange for the urgent convening of further discussions with the aim of evolving a new scheme which is not only acceptable to the two Churches as a whole, and to the present dissentients from the present scheme, but is also likely to be generally acceptable as a basis for wider unity.	108	101	4

(c) The "referendum" of the clergy (June 1969)

	Yes	No	No vote
Will you take part in the Service of Reconciliation to inaugurate Stage One?	9642	5621	243

(d) The Convocations (5–6 May 1969)

This Convocation is of the opinion that...	Yes	No	Abstentions
1. There is evidence of sufficient agreement in doctrine and practice between the two Churches for entry on Stage One, but recognizes there are problems to be resolved before entry on Stage Two to which the Church is ultimately committed by this Scheme	241	85	—
2. The proposed new Ordinal and its preface will ensure the continuance of the Catholic ministry	312	16	1
3. The Service of Reconciliation is theologically adequate to make the ministries of the two Churches mutually acceptable.	236	77	—

(e) The Convocations' Final Decision (8 July 1969)

(For this resolution to be successful it had to command an overall 75 % of those present and voting in the Four Houses, and 66⅔ % in each of the four Houses separately.)

This Convocation gives final approval to the inauguration of Stage One of the Anglican–Methodist proposals and desires the necessary legislation to be prepared in co-operation with the Methodist Church.		Yes	No	Abstentions
Canterbury	Upper House	27	2	—
	Lower House	154	77	—
York	Upper House	11	3	—
	Lower House	71	34	—
	Total	263	116	—

THE METHODIST CHURCH

All votes were simply for or against the Scheme, and abstention figures were not available

(a) The Circuit Voting (*March Quarterly Meetings*)

	Yes	No
By persons	38621	31810
By circuits	478	341

(b) The District Voting (*May Synods*)

	Yes	No
By persons	5928	2893
By districts	30	4

(c) The Conference Voting (*8 July*)

(A prior resolution had determined that the Scheme should become "Provisional Legislation" only if it attracted 75 % of those present and voting.)

Yes	No
524	153

Bibliography

The following list is not an exhaustive bibliography of our writings, but a record of those relevant to the theme of the union of the Churches, and in particular to the Anglican–Methodist Scheme.

COLIN BUCHANAN

Essays "The Service of Reconciliation" and "Ends and Means" in *The Church of England and the Methodist Church*, ed. J. I. Packer. Marcham Manor Press 1963.

Essays "Dilemmas of Unification" and "The Church of England and the Church of South India" in *All in Each Place*, ed. J. I. Packer. Marcham Manor Press 1965.

Editor of *Prospects for Reconciliation* (Northwood Christian Book Centre 1967), and essays in this volume "Retrospect to 1965", "The Service of Reconciliation", and "The Way Ahead".

Article "The Place of Ambiguity in Schemes for Reunion" in *The Churchman* (Autumn 1967).

Essay "Full Communion and the Historic Episcopate" in *Fellowship in the Gospel*, ed. J. I. Packer. Marcham Manor Press 1968.

Signatory of Evangelical Open Letter of June 1968.

Article No. 4 in *Anglican–Methodist Unity: A Symposium*, being *The Church Quarterly* (October 1968).

Joint Article (with the Bishop of Willesden) "Intercommunion: Some Interim Agreement" in *Theology* (October 1969).

Various articles from 1963 to 1969 in *The Church of England Newspaper* commenting on the Anglican–Methodist Scheme.

E. L. MASCALL

The Recovery of Unity: A Theological Approach. Longmans 1958.

Article "Episcopal–Presbyterian Relations" in *Church Quarterly Review* (January 1958).

Article "Lambeth and Unity" in *Church Quarterly Review* (April 1959).

Article "Unity and Unification" in *Theology* (January 1962).

Article "Authority and Unity" in *Clergy Review* (April 1964).

Article "Vatican II on the Church and Ecumenism: An Anglican Comment" in *New Blackfriars* (April 1965).

Article "Collegiality, Reunion, and Reform" in *Theology* (May and June 1966).

Essay in *Realistic Reflections on Church Union* (U.S.A., ed. John Macquarrie, 1967).

J. I. PACKER

Editor of *The Church of England and the Methodist Church* (Marcham Manor Press 1963), and author of essays in this "Approaching the Report", "Episcopacy" and "Where from here?".

Signatory of Evangelical Open Letter of February 1964 (reprinted in *All in Each Place* (Marcham Manor Press 1965), pp. 15–16).

Editor of *All in Each Place* (Marcham Manor Press 1965), and author of essays in this "Wanted: A Pattern for Union" and "What is Ordination?".

Article "One Body in Christ: The Doctrine and Expression of Christian Unity" in *The Churchman* (March 1966).

Member of Anglican–Methodist Unity Commission, 1965–8, and supporter of both *The Ordinal* and *The Scheme* (S.P.C.K. and Epworth 1968), except so far as explained in "A Note by the Reverend Dr J. I. Packer" (*The Scheme*, pp. 182–3).

Editor of *Fellowship in the Gospel* (Marcham Manor Press 1968), and author of essay in this "Anglican–Methodist Unity: Which Way Now?".

Essay "Relations with Roman Catholics: an Anglican Evangelical View" in *Towards Christian Unity*, ed. B. Leeming. Geoffrey Chapman 1968.

Author *Relations between English Churchmen and Roman Catholics*. Church Book Room Press 1968.

Signatory of Evangelical Open Letter of June 1968.

Article "The Church of South India and Reunion in England" in *The Churchman* (Winter 1968).

The Way Forward in Church Union. Published by the Vicar of Islington 1969.

Various articles from 1963 to 1969 in *The Church of England Newspaper*, *The Church Times*, *News Extra*, *Evangelical Magazine*, and other periodicals, commenting on the Anglican–Methodist Scheme.

THE BISHOP OF WILLESDEN

Editor of *The Unity of the Faith*—findings of a conference convened by the Bishop to comment on the interim report. Published by the Bishop of Willesden 1967.

To Every Man's Conscience. Published by the Bishop of Willesden 1968.

Article No. 3 in *Anglican–Methodist Unity: A Symposium*, being *The Church Quarterly* (October 1968).

Article "Except They be Agreed" in *The Churchman* (Autumn 1968).

Joint Article (with Colin Buchanan) "Intercommunion: Some Interim Agreement" in *Theology* (October 1969).

Articles in *The Times* (13 July 1968 and 12 July 1969).

Other articles in *The Church Times* and *The Baptist Times* in 1969.

Index

Index

Aland, Dr Kurt, 32
ambiguity, 19, 92
Anglican–Methodist relations:
Church Relations in England (1950), 106, 125; Conversations (1956–63), 125, 128, 165; Interim Statement (1958), 106, 194; Report (1963), 105–6, 110n; voting (1964–5), 12, 110, 193; Unity Commission (1965–8), 16, 22 n, 194–9; *Towards Reconciliation* (Interim Report 1967), 15, 106; Final Report (1968), 1; *The Ordinal*, 85, 121 n, 150, 170, 208–9; 2 *The Scheme*, 11, 16 nn, 20, 23 n, 38, 71, 80, 85, 105–6, 163–5, 170–3; voting (1968–9), 12, 208–11; decision on 8 July 1969, 14, 23 n, 173; resultant situation, 9, 22, 185; Anglican–Methodist Council for Unity, 15; *see also* Stage One, Stage Two, Service of Reconciliation
Apostolic Tradition, 101
Apostolicae curae, 204
appointments, of ministers *see* ordination; to ministry, 14, 139–40
Aquinas, St Thomas, 31
Archbishop of Canterbury *see* Canterbury, Archbishop of
Arianism, 101–2
Articles of Religion, Forty-two of 1553 (no. 26), 58 n; Thirty-nine of 1571, 101–4, 108, (no. 25), 55
Assam, Bishop of, 131
Athanasius, St, 9
atonement, 49–50, 186–90
Augustine, St, of Hippo, 9, 43
Aulen, Gustaf, 102
authority, of Scripture, 29–39; of Church, 65–6

baptism, 48, 191; and Church, 53–8, 178; of infants, 58 n, 60, 66–8, 144; and confirmation, 66–8, 136; baptismal confession, 98–100; paradigm of transfer of congregations, 133
Baptists, 147, 155
Barrington-Ward, Rev. S., 116–18
Barth, Dr Karl, 8, 45, 103
Bellarmine, Cardinal, 43
Berkouwer, Dr G. C., 42
Bible *see* Scripture
bishops *see* episcopacy
Bombay, diocese, 131
Brown, Rt Rev. L. W. *see* St Edmundsbury and Ipswich, Bishop of
Buchanan, Rev. Colin O., 5, 15–16, 169, 192, 212
Bulley, Rt Rev. S. C. *see* Carlisle, Bishop of

Canon Law of Church of England, reform of, 14; new Canons, 145, 164; B 12, 201–2; C 1, 83, 201–2
canon of Scripture, 32, 35–6
Canterbury, Archbishop of: Dr C. G. Lang, 181; Lord Fisher, 11, 24, 125, 129, 155, 171; Dr A. M. Ramsey, 8, 23, 50, 83 n; position in relation to united Church, 155
Carlisle, Bishop of, 13, 21
Catechism, 57–8
cathedrals, 138, 155
Catholic, Catholicism *passim*
Catholic Revival, 44
celebrant of Eucharist, 62, 81, 118, 120 n, 179; *see also* lay celebration
Ceylon (Lanka) union scheme, 132

217

Chadwick, Rev. Dr O., 31
character, 83–4, 112–13, 193–4
children, 60–1, 66–8
Church, doctrine of, 30, 34–6, 49–
68, 69–88 *passim*, 144–5, 171,
187; *see also* authority of
Church
Church of India, [Pakistan,] Burma, and Ceylon (C.I.[P.]B.C.),
130–1 n, 155, 180–1
Church of South India (C.S.I.),
111, 115–18, 130–2, 146, 148,
155, 194–5
Colquhoun, Rev. Canon F., 198 n
Communion, Holy *see* Eucharist
communion: with bishop, 67–8,
70–1, 135–6; between Churches
see intercommunion
comprehensiveness, 22–3 n, 91–3,
139
conditional ordination *see* ordination
Conference *see* Methodist Church
confession, sacramental, 30, 44
confessional statements of faith,
98–109
confirmation, 30, 66–8, 178
Congregationalist-Presbyterian
Church, 200
conscience, 19, 111–12, 116–18,
120, 206
constitution of united Church *see*
united Church
Convocations (1955), 146; (1965),
12; (1969), 13, 22 n, 161, 194,
201
Councils: Trent, 31, 43–5, 103;
Vatican I, 53 n; Vatican II, 31–2,
80, 173, 177, 183
Countess of Huntingdon's Connexion, 144, 200
"covenant", 181
Craston, Rev. Canon R. C., 140 n
creation, 40, 56, 187
Creswell, Rev. Amos, 22 n
Crown, 150
Croydon, archdeaconry, 130 n
C.S.I. *see* Church of South India

deism, 70
diaconate, 142
Didache, 191

Eastern Churches, 103, 173, 177,
193, 203
episcopacy, episcopate, 70–88, 137–
9; and initiation, 67–8; relation
to diocese, 68, 78–9, 138; to
Church, 30, 70–88, 126, 137,
157; to apostolate, 75–80; to
succession, 77–8; as proposed
for Methodism, 126–7, 167;
appointment of bishops, 143;
suffragan bishops, 76 n, 138 n;
"bishops at the customs", 199;
see also communion with bishop
eschatology, 59, 99, 173
Essays and Reviews, 92, 104
Eucharist: and Church, 58–61,
178; eucharistic presence, 30;
sacrifice, 30, 43–4, 59–60, 186–92
Evangelical, Evangelicalism *passim*
evangelism *see* mission
Every, Bro. George, 190

finance, 143, 151, 159
Fisher, Lord *see* Canterbury, Arch-
bishop of
form-critical school, 32
Free Churches *see* non-episcopal
Churches

Gnosticism, 70
Green, Rev. E. Michael B., 6, 16–
17, 25, 169, 186, 192

Hanson, Rev. Prof. R. P. C., 36
Hebert, Rev. A. G., 79
Henderson, Prof. Ian, 91
Hollis, Rt Rev. A. M., 181
Holy Communion *see* Eucharist
Hooker, Dr Morna, 16
Houlden, Rev. J. L., 83 n
Hoskyns, Sir Edwyn, 50, 69
Hubback, Rt Rev. G. C. *see*
Assam, Bishop of
Hunter, Rev. Dr A. M., 54, 100